Eat Greek for a Week

TONIA BUXTON

BLINK

bringing you closer

Eat Greek
for a Week

Published by Blink Publishing
107-109 The Plaza,
535 King's Road,
Chelsea Harbour,
London, SW10 0SZ

www.blinkpublishing.co.uk

facebook.com/blinkpublishing
twitter.com/blinkpublishing

978-1-910536-07-0

A CIP catalogue of this book is available from the British Library.

Design by Blink Publishing

Printed and bound by Interak, Poland

1 3 5 7 9 10 8 6 4 2

Papers used by Blink Publishing are natural, recyclable products made
from wood grown in sustainable forests. The manufacturing processes
conform to the environmental regulations of the country of origin.

Every reasonable effort has been made to trace copyright holders of
material reproduced in this book, but if any have been inadvertently
overlooked the publishers would be glad to hear from them.

Blink Publishing is an imprint of the Bonnier Publishing Group
www.bonnierpublishing.co.uk

GREEK FOOD IS FULL OF FRESH, VIBRANT FLAVOURS, with vegetarian and vegan dishes that make your mouth water as well as slow cooked meats and lots of fish. The cuisine truly is the best food for your palate and the most amazing food for your body. This book is a wonderful representation of both facets of Greek cooking, so much so I have separated the book into five clear diets for you to follow during the course of a week. On the following pages you will find five diets, each with its own specific ingredient colour code and nutrition list (*see* key below). The colour of each diet corresponds to the ingredients contained in each recipe and you can therefore choose to follow a certain diet as you explore the wonderful recipes contained in this book. **Eat Greek to get pregnant**; **eat Greek to manage and prevent diabetes**; **eat Greek to look and feel younger**; **eat Greek to increase your libido** and **eat Greek to reach your ideal weight** – each diet is tailor-made to suit your own lifestyle while incorporating some of the most amazing ingredients from the south eastern corner of Europe.

Indeed, the ingredients in my recipes are not set in stone; if you do not like ground coriander, then take it out and add cumin instead. If you prefer less garlic or more, go with your own taste preferences – experiment with the recipes and most of all have fun doing it.

Here are a few pieces of advice that would be good to adhere to if you can: wherever you can afford it, buy organic. Unlike 20 years ago, organic produce is readily available in most products. There is no point in following a healthy diet if it is full of pesticides and fertilisers. Some things must be organic; anything grown under the ground, like carrots or potatoes, absorbs much more of the toxic chemicals, the same for anything soft-skinned like tomatoes and berries. Non-organic chicken, especially the breast, is full of hormones which really affect our bodies in a negative way, so it really must be organic. Never use anything white, it is just sugar – so no white pasta, or rice or sugar, it all tastes so much better brown or wholemeal anyway, keeps you full and the fibre clears your insides of toxins too.

Only use Greek olives as they truly are the best in the world. I adore Kalamarta olives with their variation of hues from black to purple to brown, as they should look, (unlike Spanish black olives, for example, which are all pitch black because they are artificially dyed). The best olive oil also comes from Greece and Cyprus. For salads and eating raw use low acidity extra virgin, but if using to cook, virgin olive oil is fine.

The whole world knows how wonderful Greek yogurt is. I use many different brands and luckily most supermarkets stock Total Greek yogurt, it really is one of the best, and if you are on the Ideal Weight plan you have the option to use the 2% or 0% if you like.

This is a Greek recipe book, but if you don't fancy cooking, many of my recipes can be found at **The Real Greek** restaurants, where I am consulting executive chef and constantly coming up with seasonal choices or specials. Actually if you mention when ordering your meal you have my book you will get **10% off your food bill** – now that's Greek Filoxenia for you!

Key to Colour Coding: ● Ideal Weight   ● Manage and Prevent Diabetes

● Look and Feel Younger   ● Libido

● Pregnancy

CONTENTS

INTRODUCTION

Tʜɪs ʙᴏᴏᴋ ɪs ғɪʀsᴛ ᴀɴᴅ ғᴏʀᴇᴍᴏsᴛ ᴀ ʟᴏᴠᴇʟʏ ʀᴇᴄɪᴘᴇ ʙᴏᴏᴋ, full of delicious recipes for you to cook for yourself, friends and family. As a by-product of cooking food from this book, you will feel wonderful, look great, have lots of energy and heal yourself.

My experience of eating Greek has shown me that by eating good food and living an active life I can not only look younger but I can also feel younger and I truly believe that I have, by living this lifestyle, prevented getting certain illnesses that I was genetically predestined to get. Both my parents have had varicose veins, which has a very strong genetic link – I have not. High blood pressure is on both sides of my family and I have perfect blood pressure.

Every recipe contributes to each weekly diet. If, for example, you wish to look younger, but follow the **getting pregnant plan** or the managing **diabetes plan**, you will still be on the road to looking and feeling younger, as all the recipes are good for you, provide the best, fresh nutrition, and will have positive effects on your life. The only 'weeks' that require a little more care are the **ideal weight plan** and the **manage diabetes plan**. The detail for each week – including nutritional information and how to gain optimum results – can be found in the pages after each weekly diet.

When I say eat Greek for a week, I mean eat Greek forever if you want to feel well, look young and have lots of energy and be healthy. It has been proven again and again in study after study that the Mediterranean diet is the best, and the best of all the diets of the Med is the Greek. You really do not need to be a scientist to understand why; the Greek diet is full of vegetables, fruits, pulses and lots of olive oil. This is no faddy, cutting-out-whole-food-groups plan or expecting-you-to-starve-for-long-periods diet. It is a way of eating and living that has been proved to work.

'Ola pan Metron' wrote Aristotle – 'everything with moderation'.

Eating should be a joy, not a chore, and we should eat to feed our bodies and our minds with the nutrients we need to lead happy, productive lives. Eating well is so important, it affects the whole of our lives; if you eat a diet that is processed, full of toxins like hydrogenated fat, fructose-glucose sugars, fertilisers and pesticides you WILL get sick, but before you get sick, you will become unhappy, bloated and have less energy. You will start to look older than your years and you will start to be old in your mind too. The Greek diet is a naturally alkaline diet: it will help you slow down the signs of ageing, encourage weight loss, reduce bloating and constipation, renew your energy and vitality; it will improve your mood and help you think clearly; it will increase your fertility, defend you from disease and you will thoroughly enjoy cooking and eating delicious food!

I enjoyed writing these recipes and hope you enjoying preparing and eating them. The point to life is to be happy – so be happy, love life and eat good food.

Filakia xxxx

Tonia

'There is a fountain of youth, and it's Greek'

– Kypros Constantinou

I BELIEVE THE PROOF IS IN THE PUDDING, as the saying goes, and when you ask people who look great and have great energy what type of lifestyle they have, it is often exactly like the Greeks.

Before I go into all the good stuff I first need to go over what you *shouldn't* be doing. First: DON'T SMOKE. IF YOU DO, GIVE UP NOW! There is just no point to it, just stop – it makes you sick, it makes you look old and it makes you smell awful! There are so many medical facts as to why you should not smoke, I'm not going to go over them here, but needless to say there is no way you can look good past your 30s if you do. Can you tell how passionate I am about this?

The other thing not to do is drink too much – a glass of wine or two a few times a week is fine but any more than that will cease being medicinal and the effects will ravage your face and body. I am a child of the 1980s and boy did we worship the sun then. We didn't know about Sun Protection Factors (SPFs) and the damage the sun can do. But we do now, so always wear a high SPF, even in cloudy weather, and I recommend not sunbathing, it will make you look older in the long run.

You do need to help your diet with some moderate exercise to get the blood flowing and to keep you supple. I try and raise my heart rate two or three times a week with brisk walking, jogging and sprinting. Then as we get older our muscles atrophy so it is very important to do something to prevent that – perhaps push weights or go to a pump class, one or two times a week. Finally, to keep supple, you should try to stretch every day, or go to a yoga or a Pilates class.

Work at being happy and surround yourself with people who are fun – nothing enhances youth more than a young spirit.

Now, how to eat. Nutrition is the best place to start when you are working towards looking younger because, here's the pun, it is more than skin deep. What you put into your body has deep ramifications. One way we age is when the oxidants in our system start to break down our fibres and collagen. Think of it as rusting – oxidants cause our bodies to stiffen up and rust. Antioxidants are what prevent this from happening; they keep us smooth, oiled and supple.

The secret to looking and, in fact, feeling younger is very achievable through your diet; all you need to do is do what the healthy people of the Mediterranean have been doing for centuries and eat Greek! Changes to your diet can have great improvements not only on your skin, but also on your entire well-being. Something as simple as increasing the antioxidants in your body can make a visible difference, which you and all those around you will notice.

The Greek diet is especially effective when trying to look and feel younger. The ingredients used to create the dishes will not only complement each other with anti-ageing properties such as antioxidants and essential fats which keep your skin elastic and your blood running efficiently with fewer free radicals, but they are quite the opposite to the foods which increase the rate of ageing, so they're twice as effective, and four times as tasty.

With each meal, you will be pouring the secrets of the Mediterranean into your body – it will be like your skin has gone on holiday and forgot to write you a postcard! If you are anything like me, you will want to stop reading and start cooking yourself younger! The journey begins in your kitchen.

NUTRIENT	WHAT IT DOES	FOOD FOR OPTIMUM RESULTS
Vitamin A	• Several beneficial factors for keeping the skin looking and functioning healthily including smoothness, firmness and texture. • Used in treatment for several conditions including severe acne and psoriasis. • Produces and protects the oils for healthy hair and scalp. • Deficiency leads to scaly skin, rough and dry skin and suppression of mucus secretion and hair loss. • Boosts immune function. • Aiding in healthy vision.	Olive oil, liver, kidney, egg yolk, sweet potato, carrots, kale, butternut squash, cos and romaine lettuce, dried apricots, cantaloupe melon, red peppers, tuna, mango, cheese, yogurt.
Vitamin B6	• Essential for the creation of the substance that carries oxygen around the body (haemoglobin).	Tuna, turkey, lean pork, lean beef, liver, salmon, cod, bananas, spinach, bell peppers, turnip greens, collard greens, garlic, cauliflower, celery, cabbage, asparagus, broccoli, kale, avocado, Brussels sprouts, pistachio, sunflower seeds.
Vitamin C	• Involved in collagen production. • Antioxidant for the skin. • Strengthens immune system. • Protects the skin from sun damage. • Keeps hair follicles healthy.	Bell peppers, citrus fruits, dark green leafy veg, kale, kiwi, broccoli, berries, cooked tomatoes, peas, guava, pineapples.
Vitamin D	• Helps cell growth, hair growth and bone development. • Keeps a healthy immune system. • Deficiency leads to poor hair growth, increased cancer risk, bone failure and weakening of the muscles.	Eggs, oily fish, caviar, dairy, mushrooms, extra lean pork, cereal.

NUTRIENT	WHAT IT DOES	FOOD FOR OPTIMUM RESULTS
Vitamin E	• Acts as a guard for the cell membrane, protecting what enters and exits the cells. • Reduces moisture loss. • Combined with vitamin C, protects against UV harm. • Reduces risk of age-related eye damage (macular degeneration). • Reduces heart disease by oxidation of the blood and reduces chance of clots. • Reduces chronic inflammation. • Found to reduce risk of dementia. • Acts as an antioxidant in the stomach and may reduce cancer risk.	Olive oil, wheatgerm, sunflower seeds, peanuts, almonds, avocados, spinach, shrimp, rainbow trout, butternut squash, pumpkin.
Iron	• Essential for transportation of oxygen to all parts of the body. • Deficiency leads to pale skin, fatigue, weakness and even organ failure.	Molluscs, liver, spinach, beans and pulses, sesame seeds, squash and pumpkin seeds (raw), venison, beef, lean lamb, nuts, egg yolk, whole grains, leafy greens, dark chocolate, berries, apricots, grapes.
Selenium Increases the effectiveness of vitamin E, so double antioxidant effect. Organic is most beneficial as it has been found to contain more nutrients than non-organic food	• Protects the skin's quality and elasticity. • Protects the skin against the sun. • Antioxidant which fights age-related disease by protecting the cells from free radical damage. • Deficiency associated with premature ageing. • Relieves hot flushes and other menopause symptoms. • Reduces risk of heart attack, stroke and cancer. • Increases good cholesterol and decreases bad cholesterol.	Brazil nuts, oysters, tuna, salmon, cod, halibut, shrimp, wheatgerm, brown rice, lean pork, beef, lamb, chicken, turkey, liver, mushrooms, rye, eggs.
Zinc	• Aid in tissue repair and regeneration. • Promotes wound healing. • Deficiency leads to hair loss and flaky scalp. • Increases vitamin A in the blood by aiding transportation.	Tahini, yogurt, spinach, pumpkin seeds, sesame seeds, cashews, bran flakes, wheatgerm, lentils, calf liver, oysters, beef, lamb, lean pork shoulder, chicken, venison, turkey, green peas, beans, shrimp, chocolate, mushrooms.

NUTRIENT	WHAT IT DOES	FOOD FOR OPTIMUM RESULTS
Omega-3 Get it from your diet, not from fish oil capsules as they can thin the blood!	• Keeps the skin lubricated. • Keeps maintenance and strength of hair. • Keeps cell membranes at their optimum so they keep harmful toxins out of the skin as well as keeping the cells supple and flexible. • Protects against sun damage.	Wild Salmon, mackerel, sardines, tinned tuna, halibut, shrimp, snapper, fish roe, scallops, oysters, flax seed and oil, walnuts, red peppers.
Fats Unsaturated	• Contain polyphenols, powerful antioxidants that may help prevent age-related diseases. • Help your skin stay hydrated. • Aid absorption of vitamins and nutrients that your skin needs for optimum health.	Olive oil, nuts, seeds, fish, organic meats, avocado, macadamia nut oil.
Protein	• A building block for skin and collagen. • Essential for strong hair. • Aids muscle growth, especially after damage. • Essential for growth and function of the human body.	Turkey breast, chicken breast, tuna, salmon, halibut, cheese, pork loin, lean beef and veal, beans, eggs, yogurt, nuts and seeds.
Beta-carotene Olive oil helps the absorption of beta-carotene!	• Essential for skin health • Converts to Vitamin A, which is vital for cell repair and growth. • Powerful antioxidant found to assist healthy ageing and protect against cancer.	Sweet potato, carrots, pumpkins, cantaloupe melon, Swiss chard, spinach, kale, cos or romaine lettuce, butternut squash, red peppers, peas, paprika, chilli, parsley, coriander, cayenne.

NUTRIENT	WHAT IT DOES	FOOD FOR OPTIMUM RESULTS
Magnesium	• Keeps a healthy immune system. • Boosts energy levels. • Deficiency can lead to age-related issues including osteoporosis and high blood pressure. • Essential for every cell in the body, especially those in the heart and brain. • Deficiency can lead to mental confusion, disorientation, muscle cramps, amongst other things.	Dark leafy greens (spinach), nuts and seeds, mackerel, beans, lentils, whole grains, avocado, bananas, dried figs, dark chocolate.
Polyphenols (plant)	• Been found to reduce the risk of sun-related cancers. • Antioxidant aiding cell growth and reproduction. • Aids prevention of atherosclerosis. • Increases the body's defence, protecting against various chronic diseases including heart disease, allergies and cognitive decline.	Cloves, star anise, cocoa powder and dark chocolate, capers, black olive, green olive, hazelnut, pecan nut, plum, sweet basil, globe artichoke heads, dried ginger, apple, spinach, red wine, extra-virgin olive oil.
Water Though not a nutrient, absolutely critical! And, we can find it in our foods!	• Essential for keeping natural skin moisture, soft skin and to avoid tightness and flaking of the skin. • Reduces dry skin. Dry skin is extremely prone to wrinkling. • Deficiency leads to reduced skin elasticity. • Regulates body temperature, stopping natural sweating and lubrication of the skin. • Transports nutrients and oxygen to all cells. • Removes waste and toxins from the body, which would otherwise try to exit through the skin, causing headache, fatigue, acne and even aggravate eczema. • Prevents cells from dehydration.	Our main water source should come from drinking fresh water, but, let's have some fun with foods which have high water content: Watermelon, grapefruit, strawberries, celery, radishes, cucumber, spinach, peppers, pineapples, tomatoes, lettuce, cantaloupe melon, courgette, aubergine.

TYPE 2 DIABETES IS A MODERN EPIDEMIC. Even if you have not yet been diagnosed, if you have an unhealthy diet and lifestyle you may well be suffering some of the symptoms. What is both frustrating and amazing is that most cases of type 2 diabetes are totally preventable, and if you have been diagnosed then eating right will allow you to live a great life.

Syndrome X is a gene that predisposes you to type 2 diabetes. It is estimated that between 20 and 25% of the UK population has Syndrome X and they will not know a thing about it until it moves to type 2 diabetes – and that will most definitely happen unless they take the right steps.

Type 2 diabetes does not come around overnight, but it is often a result of a lifetime of bad habits, which have just worn down the body's capacity to help itself. Rather alarmingly we are now seeing it occur in younger people as a result of terrible diets. Of course there are always genetic factors that come into play, but we cannot solely blame genetics when we lead such unhealthy lives – full of stress, no exercise and eating a highly processed toxic diet.

Removing excess sugar and toxins from your diet forces you to get back into the kitchen and create amazing, tasty, and healthy meals. It is time you took the responsibility for both your own health, and the health of your family by making fresh, wholesome meals that will keep the symptoms of diabetes under control or prevent you from getting it in the first place.

Type 2 diabetes was once called age-onset diabetes but it can not be called that any more as we are seeing more and more children and teenagers being affected. The World Health Organisation (WHO) say that global obesity is a much bigger problem than malnourishment, and with obesity comes an increasing amount of people with type 2 diabetes. It is thought that 60% of type 2 diabetes could have been delayed or prevented through a combination of physical activity, maintaining a healthy weight by eating the right foods and not smoking.

In a nutshell, type 2 diabetes occurs when your body is unable to produce insulin sufficiently and is unable to regulate the amount of glucose in the blood.

There are some factors that can also hinder your progress – one of the main ones is stress. When you experience stress, whether emotional or physical, your body releases a stress hormone, such as cortisol or glucagon as part of its inbuilt fight or flight mechanism. This is to help us act fast, defend ourselves and think quickly. Our body sends extra glucose into the blood to enable our muscles to move fast and therefore our blood glucose rises. This is a natural reaction, but when we are under constant stress these hormones start to do damage. This raises our blood glucose levels to the point where insulin is non-effective.

THERE IS ONLY ONE LIQUID WE NEED TO SURVIVE AND THAT IS WATER! Have I shouted that loud enough? No pop or soda, no fizzy drinks, no juice; the only acceptable liquid to drink is water and the odd glass of red wine with your meal. Herbal teas are good too and no more than two cups of coffee a day.

Exercise! Exercise please! It will make such a difference to your life; it will make it so much better. You do not have to join a gym, but that's not a bad idea. You can walk, jog, skip – do whatever type of exercise you like, just get moving. It has been said that if you lead a sedentary life it is as bad as smoking, so it really is important to do some exercise. At the very minimum do 20 minutes of exercise, three times a week, that raises your heart rate.

It has been proven again and again that the Greek diet, which is rich in vegetables and pulses, fruit and fish, along with virgin olive oil and a limited consumption of red meat, is the healthiest diet in the world. Combine that with cooking from scratch and exercise and you are on the way to good health. Let food be your medicine.

NUTRIENT	WHAT IT DOES	FOOD FOR OPTIMUM RESULTS
Vitamin A	• Aids healthy vision. • Boosts immune function.	Olive oil, kale, liver, kidney, egg yolk, sweet potato, carrots, kale, butternut squash, cos and romaine lettuce, dried apricots, cantaloupe melon, red peppers, tuna, mango, cheese, yogurt.
Vitamin B1 (Thiamin)	• Enhances nerve transmission. • Required to maintain cellular function. • Deficiency leads to degeneration of the nervous system and body.	Trout, salmon, tuna, mackerel, lean pork, macadamia nuts, brazil nuts, pecans, sunflower seeds, sesame seeds, wheat bread, wheat bagel, green peas, sweetcorn, acorn squash, butternut squash, asparagus, edamame beans, navy, pink and black beans, sun-dried tomato, okra, whole wheat pasta, salami.
Vitamin B6	• Helps protect against diabetic nerve damage (neuropathy). • Regulates blood sugar. • Essential for the creation of the substance that carries oxygen around the body (haemoglobin).	Tuna, turkey, lean pork, lean beef, liver, salmon, cod, bananas, spinach, bell peppers, turnip greens, collard greens, garlic, cauliflower, celery, cabbage, asparagus, broccoli, kale, avocado, Brussels sprouts, pistachio, sunflower seeds.
Vitamin B12	• Helps treat diabetic nerve damage. • Essential for the correct functioning of the nerve cells.	Shellfish, liver, caviar, mackerel, crab, lobster, beef, lamb, cheese, eggs, fortified cereals.
Vitamin C	• Helps reduce and regulate blood sugar. • May increase glucose tolerance. • Can reduce sorbitol (harmful sugar when accumulated) levels in the blood. • Involved in the synthesis and regulation of hormones. • Strengthens blood vessels, keeping them flexible, thereby aiding blood flow. • Strengthens immune system. • An antioxidant.	Citrus fruits, peppers (red and yellow bell), dark green leafy veg, kale, kiwi, broccoli, berries, cooked tomatoes, peas.
Vitamin D	• Boosts insulin sensitivity, essential for the regulation of glucose in the blood. • Helps cell growth. • Strengthens the immune system. • Deficiency leads to weakening of the bones and muscles.	Eggs, oily fish (trout), caviar, dairy, mushrooms, extra lean pork.

NUTRIENT	WHAT IT DOES	FOOD FOR OPTIMUM RESULTS
Vitamin E	• Helps reduce and balance blood sugar. • Oxygenates the blood. • Antioxidant which prevents damage to internal structures caused by free radicals (often in those deficient in vitamin E) and reduces other diabetic complications. • High vitamin E in the blood can reduce likelihood of developing type 2 diabetes. • Increases circulation in the body. • Reduces heart disease by oxidation of the blood and reduces chance of clots. • Acts as a guard for the cell membrane protecting what enters and exits the cells.	Olives, olive oil, spinach, almonds, sunflower seeds, avocados, shrimp, rainbow trout, broccoli, butternut squash and pumpkin.
Chromium	• Improves glucose tolerance in both type 1 and type 2 diabetes. • Lowers fasting glucose levels. • Decreases insulin levels.	Whole grain, broccoli, potatoes, grape juice, oranges, lean meats, poultry, fish, beans, eggs, nuts, garlic, dried basil, apple, bananas.
Iron	• Important to maintain high levels due to diabetes induced anaemia caused by kidney and nerve damage. • Essential for transportation of oxygen to all parts of the body. • Deficiency leads to fatigue, weakness and organ failure.	Molluscs, liver, spinach, beans and pulses, sesame seeds, squash and pumpkin seeds (raw), venison, beef, lean lamb, nuts, egg yolk, whole grains, leafy greens, dark chocolate, berries, apricots, grapes.
Selenium Increases the effectiveness of vitamin E, so double the antioxidant effect.	• Can offer protection against chronic illnesses including diabetes. • Antioxidant which protects the cells from free radical damage. • Reduces risk of heart attack, stroke and cancer. • Increases good cholesterol and decreases bad cholesterol.	Brazil nuts, oysters, tuna, salmon, cod, halibut, shrimp, wheat bread, lean pork, beef, lamb, chicken, turkey, liver, mushrooms, rye, eggs.
Zinc Zinc can easily be damaged by cooking. I recommend cooked products for a higher success rate.	• Low levels of zinc are associated with higher chances of developing diabetes in some people. • Important in insulin metabolism. • Protects against viral infections. • Found to lower blood sugar levels in some type 1 cases. • Can protect some cells from destruction. • Aiding in tissue repair and regeneration as well as strengthening the immune system. • Keeps adrenal activity healthy which can fight the effects stress has on the body.	Calf liver, oysters, beef, lamb, lean pork shoulder, chicken, venison, sesame seeds, pumpkin seeds, yogurt, turkey, green peas, beans, shrimp, wheatgerm, spinach, cashews, chocolate, mushrooms.

NUTRIENT	WHAT IT DOES	FOOD FOR OPTIMUM RESULTS
Fats and Essential Fatty Acids	• Aids blood clot regulation, reducing heart attack and stroke rates. • Can lower blood pressure by significant amounts. • Omega-3 facilitates healthy blood flow and regulates hormones. • Facilitates the production of all hormones in the body. • Helps the body store more fat soluble vitamins including vitamin E. • Helps your skin and internal organs stay hydrated.	Olive oil, nuts, seeds, tinned tuna, salmon, sardines, halibut, shrimp, snapper, fish roe, scallops, oysters, mackerel, organic meats, avocado, macadamia nut oil, flax seed and oil, walnuts, red peppers.
Protein	• Provides amino acids: essential building blocks for all cells in the body. • Aids muscle growth, especially after damage.	Turkey breast, chicken breast, tuna, salmon, halibut, cheese, pork loin, lean beef and veal, beans, egg whites, yogurt, nuts and seeds, beans, sun-dried tomato.
Potassium	• Administering insulin may cause potassium deficiency: greatly important to get potassium in the diet as this will reduce the deficiency and may also improve insulin sensitivity.	Sweet potatoe, tomatoes, beetroot, green beans
Fibre	• Essential for removing excess xenohormones from the body. • Keeps a healthy digestive system maximising nutrient uptake and functionality.	Bran, cauliflower, broccoli, cabbage, berries, leafy greens, celery, squash, kidney beans, mushrooms, oranges, corn.
Lipoic Acid	• An antioxidant. • Helps the body re-use antioxidants.	Potatoes, red meat, heart, liver, kidneys, broccoli, spinach.
Beta-carotene Olive oil helps the absorption of beta-carotene!	• Powerful antioxidant. • Converts to Vitamin A, which is vital for cell repair and growth.	Sweet potato, carrots, pumpkins, cantaloupe melon, Swiss chard, spinach, kale, cos or romaine lettuce, butternut squash, red peppers, peas, paprika, chilli, parsley, coriander, cayenne.

NUTRIENT	WHAT IT DOES	FOOD FOR OPTIMUM RESULTS
Polyphenols (plant)	• Antioxidant aiding cell growth and reproduction. • Aids prevention of atherosclerosis. • Increases the body's defence protecting against various chronic diseases including heart disease. • Increases defence against allergies.	Cloves, star anise, cocoa powder and dark chocolate, capers, black olive, green olive, hazelnut, pecan nut, plum, sweet basil, globe artichoke heads, dried ginger, apple, spinach, red wine, extra-virgin olive oil.
Magnesium	• Helps glucose metabolism and diabetics are often magnesium deficient. • Magnesium deficiency linked with poor blood sugar control in type 2 diabetes, interrupted insulin secretion and increase in insulin resistance. • High levels of magnesium may lead to a lower insulin dosage needed. • Helps neutralise stomach acid and moves stools through the intestine. • Boosts energy levels. • Involved in the production of hormones and neurotransmitters. • Essential for maximum functionality of every cell in the body. • Deficiency can lead to muscle cramps amongst other things. • Essential for healthy muscle contraction.	Dark leafy greens (spinach), nuts and seeds, mackerel, beans, lentils, whole grains, avocado, bananas, dried figs, dark chocolate.
Alpha Lipoic Acid	• Can reduce and control blood sugar significantly by decreasing insulin resistance. • Can be effective for reducing nerve damage, pain, burning sensation and numbness caused by diabetes inflicted nerve damage. • Extremely powerful and versatile antioxidant. • Restores vitamin E and vitamin C levels. • Can improve the function and conduction of neurons in diabetes. • Used to break down carbohydrates into energy. • Also used to treat various eye-related disorders.	Yeast, organ meats including heart, liver and kidney, spinach, broccoli, potatoes and tomato, peas, Brussels sprouts.

SPECIFIC FOOD	WHY AND HOW IT HELPS
Fenugreek	• Slows absorption of sugars in the stomach and stimulates insulin, which lowers blood sugar. • Improves glycemic control.
Oats	• Slows absorption of sugars in the stomach and stimulates insulin, which lowers blood sugar. • Improves glycemic control. • May reduce cholesterol and blood sugar levels. • Can control appetite by causing a feeling of fullness. • Oat bran might work by blocking the absorption from the gut of substances that contribute to heart disease, high cholesterol, and diabetes.
Xanthan Gum	• Used for lowering blood sugar and total cholesterol in people with diabetes. • Swells in the intestine, stimulating the digestive tract and may be used as a laxative. • Can slow the absorption of sugar from the digestive tract.
Prickly Pear	• Contains fibre and pectin, which lower blood glucose by decreasing the absorption of sugar in the stomach and intestine. • May decrease cholesterol levels. • Can kill viruses in the body.
Ginseng (American)	• Contains ginsenosides that affect insulin levels in the body and lower blood sugar. • Fights cold and flu infection.
Ginger	• Increases glucose uptake without the use of insulin. • Helps the health of the eye.
Olive Oil	• Helps control and prevent diabetes in adults and children. • Should help lower triglicerides, improve blood sugar control and facilitate greater insulin sensitivity.
Aloe Vera	• Opens restricted blood vessels to help oxygen and nutrient transportation. • Regulates insulin flow and lowers blood glucose naturally.
Bitter Melon	• Effective way to control blood glucose by activating the AMPK enzyme, a glucose transporter.
Billberry Fruit	• Can help retinal problems associated with diabetes due to its anthocyanoside chemical. • Billberry leaf can reduce blood glucose.
Cinnamon	• Reduces glucose, triglyceride and cholesterol. • Has an important role in regulating blood sugar in people with diabetes.
Green Tea	• Helps sensitise cells, aiding better ability to metabolise sugar.
Okra (see www.diabetes.co.uk)	• Has been found to lower blood glucose in several studies. • Okra seeds have been long used as diabetes medicine in some parts of the world. • Insoluble fibre contained in okra is believed to help stabilise blood glucose by slowing the rate at which sugar is absorbed from the intestinal tract. • Okra is a rich source of dietary fibre, important vitamins and minerals, and powerful antioxidants. The vegetable is known to be beneficial for health in a number of ways including: preventing and improving constipation, lowering cholesterol, reducing the risk of some forms of cancer, especially colorectal cancer, improving energy levels and improving symptoms of depression, helping to treat sore throat, irritable bowel, ulcers and lung inflammation.

NOTHING REDUCES YOUR INTEREST IN SEX MORE THAN LOW SELF-ESTEEM. You need to spoil yourself when you're feeling down and take some time to relax or do an activity that makes you feel better within yourself. Yes, nutrition can make a huge difference to your libido, but it really does all start in the mind. Our sub-conscious mind is a minefield, but once you start getting it to work with you there is nothing you cannot achieve.

It's well known that smoking can have a terrible effect on blood flow to the sexual organs as it causes the blood vessels to narrow. It restricts blood flow and damages blood vessels, causes impotence, reduces stamina and performance, puts carbon monoxide and lead into your body, along with another 100 or so toxic substances; the body can also lose vitamins A, E and C through smoking – all of which are essential for arousal and intercourse! It also saps your stamina and most people don't like kissing an ashtray.

Moderate regular exercise will help improve blood flow to the sexual organs. In addition, exercise helps you feel good about yourself. Anything that improves self-esteem will improve libido. Also those that exercise tend to sleep better, and lack of sleep hinders performance and also stops your glands from working optimally.

Alcohol may well help you lose your inhibitions but anything more than a couple of glasses will dull the sensation of intercourse, decrease performance and can cause impotence. Caffeine can stress the adrenal glands when taken in high quantities, so it's best to keep it to one or two cups a day.

Stress is the enemy of pretty much everything but it really does work against the libido. I have gone into de-stressing detail in the 'Get Pregnant' diet, so take a look there, but there are so may ways to reduce stress – you need to take control and help yourself; no one can do it for you.

And of course to have a healthy libido you have to have good nutrition, it's all about blood flow and if you are not eating the right foods to get healthy, you will not, to put it crudely, get horny! The good news is the food is tasty, easy to prepare and while you eat this way you will be improving not just your libido but also your skin, your hair, your eyes, your health and you'll look younger too!

NUTRIENT	WHAT IT DOES	FOOD FOR OPTIMUM RESULTS
Vitamin A	• Regulates the synthesis of progesterone and testosterone. • Boosts immune function. • Aids healthy functioning of the sex organs. • Important for the health of the mucous membranes (lips, mouth, clitoris, clitoral hood, head of the penis, anus). • Lack of vitamin A can cause testicle and ovary atrophy which may lead to sterilisation. • Keeps the skin healthy.	Olive oil, kale, liver, kidney, egg yolk, sweet potato, carrots, kale, butternut squash, cos and romaine lettuce, dried apricots, cantaloupe melon, red peppers, tuna, mango, cheese, yogurt.
Vitamin B1 (Thiamin)	• Enhances nerve transmission and energy production which are essential to increase libido. • Required to maintain cellular function. • Deficiency leads to degeneration of the nervous system and body.	Trout, salmon, tuna, mackerel, lean pork, macadamia nuts, brazil nuts, pecans, sunflower seeds, sesame seeds, wheat bread, wheat bagel, green peas, sweetcorn, acorn squash, butternut squash, asparagus, edamame beans, navy, pink and black beans, sun-dried tomato, okra, wholewheat pasta, salami.
Vitamin B3 (Niacin)	• Known to increase blood flow to the skin, increasing sensitivity. • Found to increase blood flow to the clitoris and clitoral hood as well as the head of the penis, which will strengthen the orgasm for both men and women.	Tuna, mackerel, salmon, swordfish, halibut, chicken and turkey breast, lean pork, liver (lamb, beef, veal, chicken and pork), peanuts, lean beef, Portobello mushroom, green peas, sunflower seeds, chia seeds, avocado.
Vitamin B6	• Regulates hormone balance and blood sugar. • Essential for the creation of the substance that carries oxygen around the body (haemoglobin). • Controls elevated prolactin. Essential as high levels of prolactin may cause reduced sex drive and fertility in men and women, and erectile dysfunction in men.	Tuna, turkey, lean pork, lean beef, liver, salmon, cod, bananas, spinach, bell peppers, turnip greens, collard greens, garlic, cauliflower, celery, cabbage, asparagus, broccoli, kale, avocado, Brussels sprouts, pistachio, sunflower seeds.
Vitamin B12	• Low B12 linked with abnormal oestrogen levels. • Improves sperm quality and production.	Shellfish, liver, caviar, mackerel, crab, lobster, beef, lamb, cheese, eggs, fortified cereals.

NUTRIENT	WHAT IT DOES	FOOD FOR OPTIMUM RESULTS
Vitamin C	• Regulates hormones in women. • Involved in the synthesis of the hormones which cause sexual arousal. • Increases sperm count and mobility. • Strengthens blood vessels keeping them flexible, thereby aiding blood flow. • Strengthens immune system.	Citrus fruits, peppers (red and yellow bell), dark green leafy veg, kale, kiwi, broccoli, berries, cooked tomatoes, peas.
Vitamin D	• Helps the body create sex hormones, leading to hormonal balance. • Strengthens the immune system. • Deficiency leads to weakening of the bones and muscles.	Eggs, oily fish (trout), caviar, dairy, mushrooms, extra lean pork.
Vitamin E The Sex Vitamin	• Antioxidant found to help sperm and egg DNA. • Facilitates lubrication which can enhance sensation. • Reduces prostate enlargement. • Increases circulation in the body. • Increases sperm health and mobility in men. • Helps oxidation of the blood. • Reduces chronic inflammation. • An antioxidant which fights free radicals in the sex glands. • Helps menopausal symptoms. • Reduces premenstrual syndrome.	Olives, olive oil, spinach, almonds, sunflower seeds, avocados, shrimp, rainbow trout, broccoli, butternut squash and pumpkin.
Folic Acid (B9)	• Improves sperm quality. • Makes essential changes to sperm DNA which reduces the rate of birth defects.	Asparagus, liver, lentils, black-eyed peas, spinach, black beans, navy beans, kidney beans, lettuce, mango, oranges, wheat bread, chickpeas.
Iron	• Essential for transportation of oxygen to all parts of the body. • Deficiency leads to fatigue and weakness.	Molluscs, liver, spinach, beans and pulses, sesame seeds, squash and pumpkin seeds (raw), venison, beef, lean lamb, nuts, egg yolk, whole grains, leafy greens, dark chocolate, berries, apricots, grapes.

EAT GREEK TO INCREASE YOUR LIBIDO

NUTRIENT	WHAT IT DOES	FOOD FOR OPTIMUM RESULTS
Selenium Increases the effectiveness of vitamin E, so double antioxidant effect.	• Produces antioxidants which protects the sperm and egg. • Necessary for production and mobility of sperm. • Men carry up to half of the selenium in their body in their testicles and seminal ducts!	Brazil nuts, oysters, tuna, salmon, cod, halibut, shrimp, wheat bread, lean pork, beef, lamb, chicken, turkey, liver, mushrooms, rye, eggs.
Zinc Zinc can easily be damaged by cooking and I recommend the cooked products for a higher success rate.	• Required for the production of sexual hormones including testosterone. • Deficiency leads to oestrogen and progesterone imbalance. • Increases sperm levels, form, function and quality. • Aiding in tissue repair and regeneration as well as strengthening the immune system. • Zinc in the prostate gland and sperm is higher than anywhere else in the body. • Zinc keeps healthy adrenal activity which can fight the effects stress has on the body, and keep your sexual stamina high.	Calf liver, oysters, beef, lamb, lean pork shoulder, chicken, venison, sesame seeds, pumpkin seeds, yogurt, turkey, green peas, beans, shrimp, wheatgerm, spinach, cashews, chocolate, mushrooms.
Fats and Essential Fatty acids	• Omega-3 increases blood flow to the reproductive organs, regulates hormones and keeps the skin lubricated. • Facilitates the production of all hormones in the body including sex hormones like progesterone and testosterone. • Essential fatty acids (omega-3) help raise dopamine levels which trigger arousal. • Helps the body store more fat soluble vitamins including vitamin E. • Deficiency in omega-3 has been widely linked with depression. • Helps your skin and internal organs stay hydrated.	Olive oil, nuts, seeds, tinned tuna, salmon, sardines, halibut, shrimp, snapper, fish roe, scallops, oysters, mackerel, organic meats, avocado, macadamia nut oil, flax seed and oil, walnuts, red peppers.
Protein	• Provides amino acids, essential building blocks for all cells in the body. • Aids muscle growth, especially after damage.	Turkey breast, chicken breast, tuna, salmon, halibut, cheese, pork loin, lean beef and veal, beans, egg whites, yogurt, nuts and seeds, beans, sun-dried tomato.

NUTRIENT	WHAT IT DOES	FOOD FOR OPTIMUM RESULTS
Fibre	• Essential for removing excess oestrogen and xenohormones from the body. • Keeps a healthy digestive system, maximising nutrient uptake and functionality.	Bran, cauliflower, broccoli, cabbage, berries, leafy greens, celery, squash, kidney beans, mushrooms, oranges, corn.
Lipoic Acid	• Antioxidant which protects the female reproductive system. • Increases sperm quality and motility. • Helps the body re-use antioxidants.	Potatoes, red meat, heart, liver, kidneys, broccoli, spinach.
Beta-carotene Olive oil helps the absorption of beta-carotene!	• Powerful antioxidant.	Sweet potato, carrots, pumpkins, cantaloupe melon, Swiss chard, spinach, kale, cos or romaine lettuce, butternut squash, red peppers, peas, paprika, chilli, parsley, coriander, cayenne.
Magnesium	• Boosts energy levels. • Involved in the production of sex hormones and neurotransmitters which control the urge in the sex organs. • Essential for maximum functionality of every cell in the body. • Deficiency can lead to muscle cramps amongst other things. • Essential for healthy muscle contraction, therefore aids in ejaculation and orgasm.	Dark leafy greens (spinach), nuts and seeds, mackerel, beans, lentils, whole grains, avocado, bananas, dried figs, dark chocolate.

THERE ARE FAD DIETS AND THERE ARE WAYS OF LIFE, and let's clear things up right from the start, eating Greek is a *way* of life!

The purpose of reaching an ideal weight is not to lose weight, or to gain weight, but to be the healthiest weight you can be, for your age, gender and height. Believe it or not, by eating Greek, you will get closer to your ideal weight with every meal! This is because you will be eating healthy food, which work with your body's natural functionality and not against it, like many modern processed foods do.

In place of eating foods, which have been shown to increase heart disease, diabetes and many other health problems, you'll be enjoying a diet that not only tastes exquisite, but also prevents against those very same diseases, whilst keeping you healthier and stronger. Still not convinced? Cardiovascular death rates are much lower in Greece when compared to those of the UK and USA, and when smoking, drinking and other confounding variables were controlled for, diet was found to be the identifying reason for this effect.

By eating Greek, your immune system should be functioning as well as it can do, and your blood glucose will be better regulated. The other very important thing to regulate blood sugar is exercise – this diet is the best for your body but you must help it along too. Experts say that leading a sedentary diet is as bad as smoking! Our lives have changed so much since the days of our grandparents, who would on average walk 10km a day just going about their lives, so of course they did not need to make time for exercise. In today's society we must! It seems to be the thing that is last on our 'to-do' list but really it should be at the top, right next to eating right! Make time to walk more, run more, move more – you really will feel and look better for it.

The food you eat will dictate whether the weight you lose is in a healthy manner, or if, in fact, it is causing your body harm. The choice to eat Greek is about choosing a healthier way of life.

When an overweight individual follows our Greek diet, they will lose weight, not as a goal, but as a consequence of the healthy eating habits of the Greeks. Similarly, if someone who is malnourished or drastically underweight follows our diet, they should begin to see improvements in their physique too; from muscle tone to an increase in energy levels they should eventually reach their ideal weight, not as a goal, but as a consequence of maintaining a healthy body and improving the blood flow, digestion and immune system.

So what is the goal then, if becoming healthier is a consequence? To enjoy your food, by dining on mouth-watering meals that the entire family will enjoy – food that is full of natural flavour and which works with your body the way nature intended. By eating a low red meat intake, moderate chicken and fish consumption and a diet based on olive oil instead of processed, hydrogenated fats, nuts and dried fruit in place of cakes and crisps, and a high intake of fruit, vegetables and pulses and even the odd glass of red wine, you will be giving your body the tools it needs to find its balance and become your ideal weight.

NUTRIENT	WHAT IT DOES	FOOD FOR OPTIMUM RESULTS
Resistant Starch	• Reduces appetite by lowering the blood sugar spike. • Fewer calories than regular starch. • Lowers blood sugar. • Aids healthy digestion. • Improves insulin sensitivity. • Feeds friendly bacteria in the gut, increasing the number, and effectiveness, of the bacteria.	Grains, seeds, legumes, green bananas, cooked then cooled potato (perfect for salads), rye, sourdough, corn cooked and cooled, black beans, bean flakes, black-eyed peas, cashews, chickpeas, hummus, lentils, navy beans, peas, red kidney bean, red lentils, oats, vermicelli, whole rice.
Choline	• Stops fat getting blocked by the liver. • Deficiency leads to liver and kidney problems.	Egg yolk, wheatgerm, peanuts, almonds, cauliflower, broccoli, spinach, cod, chicken, grapefruit, brown rice, soya beans.
Vitamin A	• Boosts immune function.	Olive oil, kale, liver, kidney, egg yolk, sweet potato, carrots, kale, butternut squash, cos and romaine lettuce, dried apricots, cantaloupe melon, red peppers, tuna, mango, cheese, yogurt.
B Vitamins	• Keeps metabolism healthy and running efficiently. • Required to maintain cellular function. • Deficiency leads to degeneration of the nervous system and body. • Regulates blood sugar. • Essential for the creation of the substance that carries oxygen around the body (haemoglobin).	Shellfish, trout, salmon, tuna, mackerel, lean pork, macadamia nuts, brazil nuts, pecans, sunflower seeds, sesame seeds, wheat bread, wheat bagel, green peas, sweetcorn, acorn squash, butternut squash, asparagus, edamame beans, navy, pink and black beans, sun-dried tomato, okra, wholewheat pasta, salami, turkey, lean pork, lean beef, liver, cod, bananas, spinach, bell peppers, turnip greens, collard greens, garlic, cauliflower, celery, cabbage, broccoli, kale, avocado, Brussels sprouts, pistachio.
Vitamin C	• Converts glucose into energy, otherwise stored in your body. • Helps reduce and regulate blood sugar. • Involved in the synthesis and regulation of hormones. • Strengthens blood vessels keeping them flexible, thereby aiding blood flow. • Strengthens the immune system. • An antioxidant.	Citrus fruits, peppers (red and yellow bell), dark green leafy veg, kale, kiwi, broccoli, berries, cooked tomatoes, peas, blackcurrants.

NUTRIENT	WHAT IT DOES	FOOD FOR OPTIMUM RESULTS
Vitamin D	• Helps you store less fat. • Can aid in eating less but feeling satisfied longer. • Can aid fat burning of the belly and aid in healthy weight loss. • Essential for the regulation of glucose in the blood. • Helps cell growth. • Strengthens the immune system. • Deficiency leads to weakening of the bones and muscles.	Eggs, oily fish (trout), caviar, dairy, mushrooms, extra lean pork.
Vitamin E	• Helps reduce and balance blood sugar. • Oxygenates the blood. • Antioxidant which prevents damage to internal structures caused by free radicals. • Increases circulation in the body. • Reduces heart disease by oxidation of the blood and reduces chance of clots.	Olives, olive oil, spinach, almonds, sunflower seeds, avocados, shrimp, rainbow trout, broccoli, butternut squash and pumpkin.
Iron	• Essential for transportation of oxygen to all parts of the body. • Deficiency leads to fatigue, weakness and organ failure.	Molluscs, liver, spinach, beans and pulses, sesame seeds, squash and pumpkin seeds (raw), venison, beef, lean lamb, nuts, egg yolk, whole grains, leafy greens, dark chocolate, berries, apricots, grapes.
Selenium Increases the effectiveness of vitamin E, so double the antioxidant effect.	• Can offer protection against chronic illnesses. • Antioxidant which protects the cells from free radical damage. • Reduces risk of heart attack, stroke and cancer. • Increases good cholesterol and decreases bad cholesterol.	Brazil nuts, oysters, tuna, salmon, cod, halibut, shrimp, wheat bread, lean pork, beef, lamb, chicken, turkey, liver, mushrooms, rye, eggs.
Zinc Zinc can easily be damaged by cooking and I recommend the cooked products for a higher success rate.	• Protects against viral infections. • Aiding in tissue repair and regeneration as well as strengthening the immune system. • Zinc keeps healthy adrenal activity which can fight the effects stress has on the body.	Calf liver, oysters, beef, lamb, lean pork shoulder, chicken, venison, sesame seeds, pumpkin seeds, yogurt, turkey, green peas, beans, shrimp, wheatgerm, spinach, cashews, chocolate, mushrooms.

NUTRIENT	WHAT IT DOES	FOOD FOR OPTIMUM RESULTS
Fats and Essential Fatty Acids	• Aids blood clot regulation, reducing heart attack and stroke rates. • Can lower blood pressure by significant amounts. • Omega-3 facilitates healthy blood flow and regulates hormones. • Facilitates the production of all hormones in the body. • Helps the body store vitamins. • Helps your skin and internal organs stay hydrated.	Olive oil, nuts, seeds, tinned tuna, salmon, sardines, halibut, shrimp, snapper, roe, scallops, oysters, mackerel, organic meats, avocado, macadamia nut oil, flax seed and oil, walnuts, red peppers.
Protein	• Provides amino acids, essential building blocks for all cells in the body. • Aids muscle growth, especially after damage.	Turkey breast, chicken breast, tuna, salmon, halibut, cheese, pork loin, lean beef and veal, beans, egg whites, yogurt, nuts and seeds, beans, sun-dried tomato.
Fibre	• Reduces food cravings by keeping you fuller, longer. • Keeps a healthy digestive system, maximising nutrient uptake and functionality.	Bran, cauliflower, broccoli, cabbage, berries, leafy greens, celery, squash, kidney beans, mushrooms, oranges, corn.
Lipoic Acid	• An antioxidant. • Helps the body re-use antioxidants.	Potatoes, red meat, heart, liver, kidneys, broccoli, spinach.
Magnesium	• Helps neutralise stomach acid and aids healthy digestion. • Boosts energy levels. • Essential for maximum functionality of every cell in the body. • Deficiency can lead to muscle cramps amongst other things. • Essential for healthy muscle contraction.	Dark leafy greens (spinach), nuts and seeds, mackerel, beans, lentils, whole grains, avocado, bananas, dried figs, dark chocolate.
Polyphenols (plant)	• Antioxidant aiding cell growth and reproduction. • Increases the body's defence, protecting against various chronic diseases including heart disease. • Increases defence against allergies.	Cloves, star anise, cocoa powder and dark chocolate, capers, black olive, green olive, hazelnut, pecan nut, plum, sweet basil, globe artichoke heads, dried ginger, apple, spinach, red wine, extra-virgin olive oil.
Alpha Lipoic Acid	• Used to break down carbohydrates into energy. • Extremely powerful and versatile antioxidant. • Restores vitamin E and vitamin C levels.	Yeast, organ meats including heart, liver and kidney. Spinach, broccoli, potatoes and tomato, peas, Brussels sprouts.

SPECIFIC FOOD	WHY AND HOW IT HELPS
Fenugreek	• Slows absorption of sugars in the stomach and stimulates insulin, which lowers blood sugar.
Oats	• Can control appetite by causing a feeling of fullness. • May reduce cholesterol and blood sugar levels. • Oat bran might work by blocking the absorption from the gut of substances that contribute to heart disease, high cholesterol, and diabetes.
Prickly Pear	• Contains fibre and pectin, which lower blood glucose by decreasing the absorption of sugar in the stomach and intestine. • May decrease cholesterol levels. • Can kill viruses in the body.
Ginseng (American)	• Fights cold and flu infection.
Olive Oil	• Effective healthy substitute for butter and lard. • Helps control and prevent diabetes in adults and children. • Should help lower triglicerides, improve blood sugar control.
Aloe Vera	• Opens restricted blood vessels to help oxygen and nutrient transportation. • Lowers blood glucose naturally.
Cinnamon	• Reduces glucose, triglyceride and cholesterol. • Has an important role in regulating blood sugar in people with diabetes.
Green Tea	• Helps sensitise cells, aiding better ability to metabolise sugar.
Okra	• Okra is a rich source of dietary fibre, important vitamins and minerals, and powerful antioxidants, the vegetable is known to be beneficial for health in a number of ways including: preventing and improving constipation, lowering cholesterol, reducing the risk of some forms of cancer, especially colorectal cancer, improving energy levels and improving symptoms of depression, helping to treat sore throat, irritable bowel, ulcers and lung inflammation.
Avocados	• Full of fibre, protein and monounsaturated fats which can help control hunger.
Blueberries	• One cup can kill cravings by helping you feel fuller. • Fruit can help you stop craving fatty foods.
Brown rice	• Healthy carb which is a filling and low calorie alternative to white rice.
Red wine (one glass)	• Has several health benefits including a boost in calorie burning.
Kidney beans	• Protein, fibre and slimming carb-resistant starch each make this a must for any weight loss diet.
Almonds	• Several studies have found that people who eat nuts (especially almonds) as a healthy snack, lose more weight than people who indulge in regular snacks, such as crackers.
Lentils	• Boosts metabolism and burns fat.
Banana (slightly green for best results)	• Helps keep you full whilst boosting metabolism with resistant starch.
Boiled then cooled potato	• Good for weight loss and good health.
Chilli pepper	• Can aid weight loss and suppress appetite due to the capsaicin.
Grapefruit	• Found to be particularly effective when eaten before meals.
Full fat Greek yoghurt (not Greek style)	• Reduced fat yogurt is often full of sugar, and full fat can protect against inflammation whilst aiding the function of the gut. • Found to lower the risk of obesity and type 2 diabetes over time.
Cumin	• Recently discovered to aid weight loss in overweight individuals. Dieters consuming cumin daily lost three times as much body fat when compared to those who did not consume cumin.

Eat Greek for a Week… To Get Pregnant is a nutritional plan for both you and your partner. Quite simply if you make yourself as healthy and happy as you can be – both of you – then with a little love you will make a happy and healthy baby.

Let's start with what you should be avoiding. Fizzy drinks and sodas are at the top of the list of things to avoid – not just while trying to get pregnant – but because they are toxic rubbish! The same goes for trans or hydrogenated fats. Another foodstuff to avoid is high-mercury fish, such as tuna, halibut and swordfish; even the low mercury fish are best kept to one or two times a week – fish such as wild salmon or farmed trout. You should also avoid anything unpasteurised, such as certain cheeses and milk. Coffee can be drunk in moderation, but limit your intake to one or two cups a day. I believe red wine, especially organic low-sulphur red wine, is also beneficial to conceiving, but only in moderation, with a glass two to three times a week.

This is, of course, a nutrition book, but sometimes we need to be told the obvious! There are many other things to avoid if you wish to fall pregnant: studies have shown that lubricants prevent the sperm from reaching the cervical mucus and therefore they die in the acidic mucus of the vagina. Certain medications also need to be stopped, such as medicine for acne and hypertension and migraines, as they can be harmful to the foetus – but you must check with your doctor first.

It goes without saying that smoking and marijuana use are a total 'no no'. You must stop using these drugs to have a healthy baby – that goes for BOTH OF YOU! Men need to avoid hot tubs, hot baths, and cut back any heavy cycling. A man's scrotum is outside of the body for a reason – it needs to keep cool and even wearing too tight underwear can raise the temperature too much. It takes two to three months to produce mature sperm so men need too cool things down from January to enable conception in March!

The biggest enemy of conception is STRESS. I know this is a very difficult thing to deal with in today's modern living, where stress seems to be part of everyday life, but we have to try to minimise it. Stress affects every cell in your body; it affects your digestive system, your hormones and your sleep. It is very important to make time for yourself to relax, to do things you enjoy and to wind down. It is no coincidence that many babies are conceived whilst their parents are on holiday, but we can't be on holiday every day! So we have to find a way to relax without leaving the country.

Think about what makes you happy and try and make time to do that. If you can't think of anything then take ten minutes out of your day, anytime, and count your blessings; sometimes that is all you need to put things into perspective. Try to breathe well; everything starts and ends with breath, so make sure your lungs are filling and your tummy expands as you breathe in and contracts as you breathe out. Many of us shallow breathe and this, in itself, can cause stress and panic. Go online and find a relaxation technique that works for you – there are so many to choose from.

Finally, a fabulous way to get pregnant is to have lots of sex – lots and lots of it if possible. There is a common misconception that a man has to save up sperm for the right time of the month. This is not true: it is much better to have freshly made sperm, produced because of supply and demand (i.e. lots of sex) than stale sperm that has just been festering there. I know that sometimes after a long day at work sex is the last thing on your mind, but if you do want a baby you should be having sex at least three times a week.

NUTRIENT	WHAT IT DOES	FOOD FOR OPTIMUM RESULTS
Vitamin B6	• Regulates hormones and blood sugar. • Lack of B6 creates irregular menstruation. • Can help women with Luteal Phase Defect. • Eases PMS.	Tuna, turkey, lean pork, lean beef, liver, salmon, cod, bananas, spinach, bell peppers, turnip greens, collard greens, garlic, cauliflower, celery, cabbage, asparagus, broccoli, kale, avocado, Brussels sprouts, pistachio, sunflower seeds.
Vitamin B12	• Strengthens endometrial lining for egg fertilisation, decreasing risk of early miscarriage. • Low B12 linked with abnormal oestrogen levels, low ovulation and can stop ovulation. • Improves sperm quality and production.	Shellfish, liver, caviar, mackerel, crab, lobster, beef, lamb, cheese, eggs, fortified cereals.
Vitamin C	• Regulates hormones in women. • Increases sperm count and mobility, reducing miscarriage and chromosomal problems. • Can help women with Luteal Phase Defect.	Citrus fruits, peppers (red and yellow bell), dark green leafy veg, kale, kiwi, broccoli, berries, cooked tomatoes, peas.
Vitamin D	• Helps the body create sex hormones, leading to hormonal balance and ovulation. • Links between polycystic ovary syndrome (PCOS) and low Vitamin D. • Links between female infertility and vitamin D deficiency.	Eggs, oily fish (trout), caviar, dairy, mushrooms, extra lean pork.
Vitamin E	• Antioxidant found to help sperm and egg DNA. • Increases sperm health and mobility in men.	Olives, olive oil, spinach, almonds, sunflower seeds, avocados, shrimp, rainbow trout, broccoli, butternut squash and pumpkin.
Folic Acid (B9) Before and During Vital for the development of the child and should be consumed regularly whilst trying to get pregnant so that when fertilisation is successful, the developing foetus will have much of what it needs during its early development .	• Reduces ovulatory failure. • Can reduce birth defects, including neural tube defects, congenital heart defects, cleft lips, limb defects, and urinary tract anomalies in developing foetuses. • Deficiency also leads to increase in homocysteine blood levels, causing several severe pregnancy complications including spontaneous abortion.	Asparagus, liver, lentils, black-eyed-peas, spinach, black beans, navy beans, kidney beans, lettuce, mango, oranges, wheat bread, chickpeas.

NUTRIENT	WHAT IT DOES	FOOD FOR OPTIMUM RESULTS
Iron	• Lack of iron can cause low ovulation rate and poor egg health making it up to 60% harder to conceive when compared to women with adequate iron in the blood.	Molluscs, liver, spinach, beans and pulses, sesame seeds, squash and pumpkin seeds (raw), venison, beef, lean lamb, nuts, egg yolk, whole grains, leafy greens, dark chocolate, berries, apricots, grapes.
Selenium	• Produces antioxidants which protect the sperm and egg. • Prevents chromosome breakdown lowering birth defect and miscarriage rate. • Necessary for the production of sperm.	Brazil nuts, oysters, tuna, salmon, cod, halibut, shrimp, wheat bread, lean pork, beef, lamb, chicken, turkey, liver, mushrooms, rye.
Zinc Zinc can easily be damaged by cooking and I recommend the cooked products for a higher success rate.	• Deficiency leads to oestrogen and progesterone imbalance. • Low zinc linked with early miscarriage. • Increases sperm levels, form, function and quality, even in infertile men!	Calf liver, oysters, beef, lamb, lean pork shoulder, chicken, venison, sesame seeds, pumpkin seeds, yogurt, turkey, green peas, beans, shrimp, wheatgerm, spinach, cashews, chocolate, mushrooms.
Omega-3	• Regulate hormones. • Increases cervical mucus. • Promotes ovulation and quality of the uterus. • Increases blood flow to the reproductive organs. • Helps develop the baby's brain and eyes.	Tinned tuna, salmon, sardines, halibut, shrimp, snapper, fish roe, scallops, oysters, mackerel, flax seed and oil, walnuts, red peppers.
Fats Avoid hydrogenated oils and vegetable oil	• Facilitates the production of all hormones in the body including progesterone. • Helps develop the foetus.	Olive oil, coconut oil, organic meats, fish, nuts and seeds.
Protein	• Aids healthy fertility as the amino acids are essential building blocks for all cells in the body.	Chicken, turkey, fish, lean pork, lean beef, cheese, yogurt, egg white, beans, nuts and seeds, sun-dried tomato.
Fibre	• Essential for removing excess oestrogen and xenohormones from the body. • Keeps a healthy digestive system, maximising nutrient uptake and functionality.	Bran, cauliflower, broccoli, cabbage, berries, leafy greens, celery, squash, kidney beans, mushrooms, oranges, corn.
Lipoic Acid	• Antioxidant which protects the female reproductive system. • Increases sperm quality and motility. • Helps the body re-use antioxidants. • Improves cell health.	Potatoes, red meat, heart, liver, kidneys, broccoli, spinach.

THE RECIPES

BREAKFAST, BRUNCH & LIGHT BITES 40

SOUPS, SALADS & VEGETABLES 76

FISH, MEAT & POULTRY 118

PUDDINGS, BAKES & CAKES 186

BREAKFAST, BRUNCH & LIGHT BITES

Some people really can't face food in the morning, so here are some smoothies and shakes that are packed full of nutrients to help you start the day. They are also great as mid-morning or mid-afternoon snacks, or any time you need an energy kick.

WAKE UP PEAR SHAKE

If you are feeling a little sensitive, replace ginger with a handful of mint as this is super soothing on the stomach.

SERVES 4 *Ready in:* 10 minutes

4 firm conference pears, cored and chopped
2 sticks of celery, chopped
100g baby spinach leaves

1 tbsp ground almonds
A 2cm knob of root ginger, grated
Water or coconut milk to dilute (optional)

With the motor running, gradually drop the pear and celery into the blender and blitz until smooth.

Add the spinach, almonds and ginger and blend again until smooth. If you prefer to dilute the shake, trickle in a little water or coconut milk.

Pour into chilled glasses and serve immediately.

TIP:
Store your ingredients in the fridge for an instantly chilled smoothie!

HIGH ENERGY BREAKFAST SHAKE

SERVES 4 *Ready in:* 10 minutes

2 crisp dessert apples, cored and chopped
1 dessert pear, cored and chopped
2 ripe bananas, peeled

1 tbsp peanut butter
6 tbsp natural Greek yogurt
½ tsp ground cinnamon

With the motor running, gradually drop the prepared fruit into the blender and blitz.

Add the peanut butter, yogurt and cinnamon and blend again until smooth.

Pour into chilled glasses and sprinkle with a little more cinnamon if you fancy. Serve straight away.

TIP:
Store your whole apples and pears in the fridge for an instantly chilled shake!

SUPER TUMMY SMOOTHIE

SERVES 4 *Ready in:* 10 minutes

¼ cucumber
4 crisp dessert apples, cored and chopped
½ pineapple, cut into chunks, core removed

1 medium bunch fresh parsley
125ml natural Greek yogurt
½ tsp ground cinnamon

With the motor running, gradually drop the cucumber, fruit and parsley into the blender and blitz until smooth.

Add the yogurt and blend again until smooth. Pour into chilled glasses and serve immediately.

GREEK SPICED PORRIDGE

SERVES 2 *Ready in:* 10 minutes

2 cardamom pods, crushed or 1 tsp ground
    cinnamon
75g porridge oats
400ml coconut milk or coconut water or water

1 tsp rosewater
2 tbsp chopped pistachio nuts or almonds
A drizzle of runny honey
1 banana, chopped (optional)

Place the cardamom or cinnamon in a saucepan with the oats and your choice of coconut milk or water. Simmer for around 8 minutes or until the oats are tender. Add a drop more liquid if needed.

Stir in the rosewater then divide between two warm bowls, drizzle on some honey, add a sprinkling of nuts and chopped banana if you fancy. Enjoy.

PORRIDGE... MY FAVOURITE WAY

SERVES 2 *Ready in:* 10 minutes

70g porridge oats
200ml water
1 small banana, chopped

1 tsp ground cinnamon
1 tbsp chopped almonds or 5 whole almonds

Place all the ingredients in the pan and simmer slowly until cooked, for around 10 minutes.

If you like you can add a tablespoon of cream or a drizzle of honey on serving.

TIP: If making for two, take an average size mug, fill with porridge, put in the pan and then add two mugs of water and whatever else you fancy.

BUCKWHEAT PANCAKES WITH FRESH BERRY SAUCE

Pancakes are such a great food, they can be a lunch or supper or a snack, sweet or savoury. My children always love pancakes and we do not wait for it to be Shrove Tuesday to have a total pancake day. Always use wholemeal flour, then you will be getting fibre and it will be good on your blood sugar levels. Once you have mastered the basic batter, start experimenting with different fillings like pancakes with wilted spinach and crumbled feta or chopped dried figs and grated halloumi. The combinations are as big as your imagination.

SERVES 4 *Ready in:* 20 minutes

225g buckwheat flour
1 tsp baking powder
½ tsp ground cinnamon
A pinch of sea salt
275ml skimmed milk or rice milk

1 large egg, beaten
175g fresh berries i.e. strawberries, blueberries, raspberries
1 tbsp mild olive oil
A little drizzle of runny honey, to serve

In a bowl, mix together the flour, baking powder, cinnamon and salt. Add the egg and milk and beat well to form a smooth batter. Let this stand for 5 minutes or so.

Meanwhile blitz the assorted berries to form a chunky (or smoother if you wish) sauce. Cover and chill until required.

Heat a non-stick frying pan and add a few drops of olive oil. Using a 50ml ladle, swirl a couple of spoonfuls of the batter around the hot pan to make a thin pancake. Cook for 1–2 minutes then flip over and cook to brown the other side. Keep warm whilst you repeat with the remaining oil and batter to make a stack of pancakes.

Serve 3–4 pancakes per person, topped or folded with the berry sauce and a drizzle of runny honey.

PEAR AND CINNAMON MILLET

SERVES 2 *Ready in:* 20 minutes

250g millet
A pinch of sea salt
2 dessert pears, cored and sliced
1 tbsp raisins
½ tsp ground cinnamon

2 tsp wholemeal plain flour
1 tbsp toasted almonds or hazelnuts, roughly chopped
1 tbsp runny honey

Rinse the millet in cold water and drain thoroughly. Dry fry in a large frying pan for 1 minute.

Bring 375ml water to the boil in a pan. Add the millet and salt. Simmer for 10 minutes.

Now add the pear, raisins and cinnamon to the millet and simmer for a further 10 minutes.

Meanwhile, blend the wholemeal flour with a little cold water to make a smooth paste. Stir this into the millet, stirring continuously until the mixture thickens.

Divide between two warm bowls, sprinkle on the nuts and drizzle with the honey. Serve.

MAKES 8 PANCAKES / SERVES: 4   *Ready in:* 20 minutes

50g plain flour
50g gram flour, sifted
15g poppy seeds
300ml semi-skimmed milk
A pinch of salt
1 tsp sunflower oil

FOR THE FILLING:
50g chopped toasted almonds
2 ripe bananas, chopped
50g ready-to-eat dried no sulphur apricots,
  chopped
Zest and juice of 1 lemon
150ml natural Greek yogurt
1 tsp poppy seeds

Blend the flours, poppy seeds, milk & salt in a food processor then leave to stand for 20 minutes (or whisk by hand until you form a smooth batter).

Meanwhile mix together the almonds, banana, apricots and lemon juice.

Heat a non-stick frying pan and add a few drops of the oil. Use a 50ml ladle to swirl enough batter around the pan to form a thin pancake. Cook for 1–2 minutes then flip over and cook to brown the other side.

Layer the pancakes to keep warm whilst you repeat with the remaining oil and batter to make 8 pancakes.

Fill each pancake with 2tbsp of the chopped fruit and nuts then fold into quarters. Arrange two pancakes on each plate with a spoonful of thick creamy yogurt alongside, sprinkling with the poppy seeds and the lemon zest.

GARDEN HERB OMELETTE

SERVES 1 *Ready in:* 10 minutes

1 tsp butter
2 medium organic/free-range eggs, beaten
1 tbsp freshly chopped parsley

1 tbsp freshly snipped chives
A pinch of sea salt

Melt the butter in a small frying pan. Mix the eggs with 1 tbsp. cold water and a pinch of salt. As soon as the butter is turning a nutty brown colour, pour and swirl the eggs around the pan.

Use a wooden spatula to flip the outer edges of the omelette to the centre to create a light omelette. Once it is nearly setting, sprinkle over the herbs.

Slide the omelette out onto a warm plate, flipping it in half to sandwich the filling. Leave to set for 30 seconds or so. Serve immediately.

SCRAMBLED EGGS ON RYE BREAD WITH SPINACH AND ROASTED TOMATOES

SERVES 4 *Ready in:* 1 hour

4 organic ripe tomatoes, halved
6 medium free-range eggs
125ml milk
150g tender spinach leaves, torn if large

4 slices rye bread, toasted
Sea salt and freshly ground black pepper
Olive oil for drizzling

Place the tomatoes cut side up, on a baking tray. Drizzle with a little oil and season with salt and pepper. For best flavour, roast in a preheated oven (180°C/fan 160°C/gas 4) for 30–40 minutes. For a short cut, simply grill under a moderate heat.

Beat the eggs and milk together, seasoning to taste.

Heat a non-stick pan on high and add the spinach and a few sprinkles of water. Cook for 2–3 minutes to wilt the spinach. Drain off any excess water.

Now stir in the eggs and mix with the spinach, to scramble and lightly cook the eggs.

Pile each slice of toast with the egg and spinach scramble and top with two halves of tomato. Just another drizzle of olive oil and some freshly ground black pepper… and enjoy.

SCRAMBLED EGGS WITH COURGETTE AND TURMERIC

Scrambled eggs and omelettes are such a wonderfood snack/lunch. Eggs are such a great source of protein, they are one of the most nutritious foods on the planet, containing a little bit of almost every nutrient we need. You can have so many different variations and these are some of my favourites.

SERVES 4 *Ready in:* 10 minutes

2 tbsp olive oil
1 tbsp butter
½ tsp turmeric

2 courgettes (grated)
5 organic free-range eggs, lightly beaten
A pinch of sea salt

Heat the butter and fry the turmeric for a minute then add the olive oil.

Stir in the courgettes and cook for 1–2 minutes.

Add the eggs and stir till cooked, but do not over cook! Season.

Eat alone or on a slice of toasted rye or spelt bread.

GREEK YOGURT...WITH EVERYTHING

Greek yogurt is such an amazing wonder-food and it really does set you up for the day. Here are some ways to enjoy it at breakfast, but really you can go with whatever you have to hand in the cupboard, fridge or fruit bowl.

A SAVOURY START:
100ml plain Greek yogurt
½ small cucumber, chopped
2 Kalamata olives, pitted and quartered
2 ripe tomatoes, finely chopped

1 tbsp freshly chopped mint
½–1 clove garlic – *especially good if feeling a little run down*
Sea salt and freshly ground black pepper, to season

Simply spoon the yogurt into a bowl and layer on the vegetables. Spoon in and enjoy.

A SWEET START:
100ml plain Greek yogurt
1 banana, chopped/1 apple, cored and chopped, 3 strawberries, sliced

OR
1 pear, cored and sliced/4 blackberries/1 small orange, segmented
50g chopped or flaked toasted almonds
½ tsp ground cinnamon
1 tsp Greek mountain honey

Layer your yogurt with your choice of fruits and nuts, add a sprinkling of cinnamon then finish with a drizzle of honey.

EASY SPEEDY HUMMUS

MAKES A GOOD BOWLFUL *Ready in:* 20 minutes

3–6 garlic cloves
400g can chickpeas, drained, brine reserved
3 heaped tbsp tahini
Juice of 2–3 lemons
Zest of 1 lemon

2 tbsp olive oil
A pinch of sea salt
A little olive oil for drizzling

FOR THE METHOD USING A BLENDER OR FOOD PROCESSOR
Finely chop the garlic and then add the drained chickpeas and blitz until a rough texture, adding a little brine to slacken.

Add the tahini paste and then the juice of 2 lemons. Season well with salt and give the whole mix another short blitz. Adjust the flavour levels with a squeeze of lemon or a pinch of salt. Cover and chill.

FOR THE METHOD BY HAND
Crush the garlic and place in a large bowl with the drained chickpeas. Use a potato masher to crush them together.

In a separate bowl beat together the tahini paste, lemon juice and salt. Now mix into the chickpeas. Cover and chill the hummus until ready to serve

TO SERVE
Drizzle a little olive oil over the hummous and garnish with a few whole chickpeas and the lemon zest. Keep in an airtight container in the fridge for up to a week.

VARIATION
Add ½ tsp of either cumin or ground coriander for a warming flavour, or for more heat, sprinkle with finely chopped chilli or some ground paprika.

SPINACH & YOGURT DIP

1 kg fresh young spinach, chopped finely
½ large bunch fresh mint leaves, chopped
5 large spring onions, trimmed, sliced finely
¼ tsp turmeric

2 glasses (500ml) strained natural Greek yogurt
6 tbsp olive oil
Salt and freshly ground black pepper

In a large pan gently heat 3 tbsp olive oil. Add the spinach, tossing to coat the leaves with oil then leave for a couple of minutes to wilt in the heat.

Remove from the heat and tip into a bowl.

Season with salt and pepper then add the mint, spring onions, turmeric and yogurt, folding together thoroughly. Spoon into a serving bowl then drizzle on the remaining olive oil.

Serve at room temperature and eat as fresh as possible.

TAHINI DIP

This is my favourite dip, and if the truth be known I would have it accompany everything I eat – from keftedes to souvlakia to fish, or on top of plain steamed veg. As far as I am concerned it works with them all!

2 heaped tbsp of tahini paste
2–4 cloves garlic crushed
juice of 2–3 lemons
2 tbsp of olive oil
Sea salt
Cold water to thin
Chopped parsley to garnish
Generous pinch of salt to taste

YOGURT TAHINI DIP
1 heaped tbsp of wholemeal Tahini paste
2 cloves garlic, crushed (or more if you like)
A pinch of sea salt
Juice of 1 lemon
50g (1 large tbsp) Total Greek yogurt
Cold water to slacken if needed

Combine all the ingredients, beating hard (this is best done with an electric blender).

Add enough water to give a pouring consistency.

To serve sprinkle with parsley and drizzle with olive oil.

AUBERGINE DIP

SERVES 6 *Ready in:* 50 minutes plus cooling time

1 large aubergine
100ml extra-virgin olive oil
3 small onions, finely chopped
4 garlic cloves, crushed

4 tbsp red wine vinegar
Juice of 1 lemon
Sea salt and freshly ground black pepper, to taste

Preheat the oven to 200°C/fan 180°C/gas 6. Pierce the aubergine with a sharp tipped knife and place on a baking tray in the oven for 45 minutes or until the skin has wrinkled and the aubergine collapsed.

Slit the aubergine open, scoop the pulp out into a bowl and discard the skin. Roughly chop the pulp, then add the remaining ingredients. Using a hand blender, blitz until very smooth, or for a more rustic dip, roughly chop by hand.

Adjust the seasoning to taste. Serve at room temperature.

BAKED PITAKIA WITH FETA, FIG AND ROCKET

SERVES 4 *Ready in:* 30 minutes

4 round wholemeal pitta breads
1 tbsp olive oil
2 red onions, finely sliced
4 fresh figs, sliced or quartered

100g feta cheese, crumbled
Fresh sprigs of thyme
50g fresh rocket leaves

Preheat the oven to 180°C/fan 160°C/gas 4. Place the pittas on a flat baking sheet.

Heat the olive oil in a pan, add the onions and cook gently for 5 minutes or until softened and coloured.

Top each pitta with some onion. Arrange the figs on top. Sprinkle the feta over the figs and finish with sprigs of fresh thyme.

Bake in the oven for 15 minutes or until the feta is tinged golden. Serve hot with a scattering of fresh rocket leaves.

ANARI BRUSCHETTA WITH CRUSHED TOMATOES AND OLIVES

MAKES 4 *Ready in:* 20 minutes

250g cherry tomatoes
4 tbsp extra-virgin olive oil plus extra for drizzling
12 stoned Kalamata olives
2 tsp capers
4 anchovy fillets, finely chopped

4 slices of sourdough bread
200g anari cheese (use low fat ricotta if you cannot find anari)
A handful of wild rocket, basil or flat leaf parsley
Sea salt and freshly ground black pepper, to season

Roughly crush the tomatoes and toss with the olive oil, olives, capers, anchovy fillets and a little salt and pepper, to taste.

Toast the bread, drizzle with a little olive oil then spread each slice thickly with 2 tbsp anari cheese.

Pile the tomato mixture on top and garnish with fresh summer herbs or peppery leaves like basil or rocket. Enjoy.

This is a wonderful way to use a glut of tomatoes (of which there's a surplus in Greece over the summer!). It is delicious as part of a meze or just good on its own with wholemeal village bread.

SERVES 4 *Ready in:* 2 hours 15 minutes

450g tomatoes on the vine, halved
3 garlic cloves, crushed
3 tbsp extra-virgin olive oil
4 sprigs fresh thyme
40g fresh breadcrumbs
50g pine nuts

1 tbsp freshly chopped flat leaf parsley
1 tbsp freshly snipped chives
50g feta
Sea salt and freshly ground black pepper, to
    season

Preheat the oven to 120°C/fan 100°C/gas 2. Arrange the tomatoes cut side up on a roasting tray. Mix the garlic with the 2 tbsp olive oil, brush over the tomatoes then season with a little salt and pepper.

Thread the thyme leaves off their stalks over the tomatoes. Now cook for 1½–2 hours or until very soft, slightly wrinkled.

Heat the remaining tablespoon of olive oil in a large non-stick frying pan and fry the breadcrumbs for 1–2 minutes or until golden then add the pine nuts and continue to cook for a further minute to toast the nuts and crisp the crumbs. Remove from the heat.

Stir through the herbs. Spread two-thirds of the crumb mix over the base of a serving dish or individual plates, top with the tomatoes and sprinkle the remaining crumb mix over the top, then finish with crumbled feta.

TIP
Prepare the tomatoes well ahead and store in a lidded container, then bring to temperature and gently warm through before progressing at stage 3.

ANCHOVY, SUN-DRIED TOMATO AND AVOCADO OPEN SANDWICH

....

SERVES 4 *Ready in:* 5 minutes

3–5 plump garlic cloves, crushed
200g anchovies in wine vinegar
100g sun-dried tomatoes
1 ripe avocado, cut into chunks

1 small bunch fresh basil leaves
Juice of 1 lemon
2 tbsp extra-virgin olive oil
4 slices of rye bread, lightly toasted

Gently combine all the ingredients (apart from the bread) together. Season with some freshly ground black pepper.

Pile the mixture onto the toasted rye, finishing with another grind of black pepper. Serve.

SAVOURY FETA AND OREGANO MUFFINS

....

MAKES 4 *Ready in:* 40 minutes

1 onion, chopped
2 small courgettes, diced
5 tbsp olive oil
2 free-range eggs, beaten

1tsp freshly chopped oregano
150g feta cheese, crumbled
150g wholemeal flour
1½ tsp baking powder

Preheat the oven to 180°C/fan 160°C/gas 4. Line a muffin tray with 8–10 muffin cases.

Heat 2 tbsp olive oil in a frying pan then gently cook the onions and courgettes for 5 minutes or until just softened.

In a large bowl, mix the eggs with the remaining oil, the oregano and feta cheese. Add the milk, stir well then briskly fold in the flour and baking powder. Fold in the onion and courgette.

Divide between the muffin cases then bake for 20–25 minutes or until well risen, coloured and firm to the touch. Eat warm or freshly baked.

SWEET CHILLI MUSHROOMS WITH HALLOUMI CHEESE

SERVES 4 AS A STARTER OR 2 AS A LIGHT MEAL *Ready in:* 30 minutes

8 flat mushrooms
4 tbsp chilli-flavoured or extra-virgin olive oil
150g halloumi cheese, sliced into 8

FOR THE DRESSING:
1 tbsp honey
A small pinch of chilli
1 tbsp balsamic vinegar
Sea salt and black pepper
Rocket salad leaves, to serve

Heat the grill to high. Place the mushrooms gill-side up on a grill rack, brush all over with the oil and season with salt and ground black pepper. Cook under the grill for 5 minutes until the juices start to run.

Mix the dressing ingredients together and set aside.

Top with the halloumi cheese slices then return to the grill and cook for a further 4–5 minutes until the cheese is golden and crisp.

Arrange two on each of four serving plates and spoon a little of the dressing over each. Serve with the salad leaves.

CHEAT'S SPEEDY COURGETTE AND FETA PIZZA

SERVES 4 *Ready in:* 30 minutes

1 tbsp olive oil
2 cloves garlic, chopped
400g can organic chopped tomatoes
A handful of basil leaves
4 round wholemeal flatbreads

1 medium courgette, diced
1 red pepper, diced
2–3 spring onions, sliced
100g feta cheese
Freshly ground black pepper, to season

Preheat the oven to 200°C/fan 180°C/gas 6. Have ready 2 flat baking sheets.

Place the olive oil and garlic in a pan and gently heat. Add the chopped tomatoes and basil then bring to a steady simmer and cook for 15 minutes or until the mixture becomes nice and thick.

Spread the tomato sauce over each flatbread, scatter on the chopped vegetables and crumble on the feta.

Bake for 10 minutes or until tinged golden.

SPANAKOPITA

Puritans would make their own filo pastry but I think life is too short. This recipe does not use too much feta but if you prefer something a little richer put in the whole pack of feta (250g). This can be served straight out of the oven but I always like it once it has cooled and all the flavours are set. I have made it in a dish but you can also make little spanakopita parcels or triangles for parties.

SERVES 4–6 *Ready in:* 1 hour

6 tbsp olive oil
1 bunch spring onions, trimmed and finely chopped
1kg fresh spinach, washed and chopped
100g feta cheese, crumbled

2 eggs, lightly beaten
2 tbsp freshly chopped parsley
½ tsp grated nutmeg
350g filo pastry (around 8–10 sheets)
Salt and freshly ground black pepper

Heat 2 tbsp oil in a large pan or wok and fry the spring onions for a few minutes to soften without browning. Then add the drained spinach, tossing until it begins to wilt. Cover and cook gently for 5 minutes.

Allow the spinach to cool a little before mixing in the feta, eggs, parsley, nutmeg and salt and pepper to taste.

Preheat the oven to 180°C/fan 160°C/gas 4.

Brush some oil over the base of a large deep baking tin or oven dish, approx. 30cm x 25cm.

Lay 4 or 5 sheets of filo pastry in the bottom of the dish, brushing between each layer with oil. Spoon the spinach filling on top and cover with the remaining filo sheets brushing each with oil as before. Tuck in the edges neatly and brush the last of the oil over the pie.

Bake for approx. 40 minutes then increase the heat and bake for another 5 minutes to crisp the top. Serve hot or cold.

I find that mix of salty cheese and sweet honey always hits the spot or as a dessert if using unsalted cheese. These little parcels of heaven are one of my favourite things to eat. You can serve them as a starter if using salted anari (or feta cheese).

MAKES 4 *Ready in:* 40 minutes

8 leaves filo pastry
5 tbsp olive oil
4 tbsp Greek thyme honey

2 tbsp sesame seeds
300g anari cheese (use low fat ricotta if you
    cannot find anari)

Preheat the oven to 180°C/fan 160°C/gas 4.

Place one sheet of filo pastry on a large baking sheet. Brush with olive oil then lay another sheet directly on top. Place a spoonful of cheese in the centre of the pastry, drizzle ½ tsp honey on top then sprinkle lightly with some sesame seeds.

Fold over the filo pastry to encase the cheese, making a secure parcel. Brush again with oil. Repeat to make 4 parcels spaced evenly out onto the tray. Bake in the oven for 20–30 minutes or until golden.

Transfer the hot parcels onto individual plates, halve and drizzle with a little honey, scatter on some sesame seeds and serve.

YALAJI RICE AND SULTANA STUFFED VINE LEAVES

Yalaji, dolmades or koubebia are all basically little cigarillo shapes that are stuffed vine leaves. These ones are vegan but there are so many wonderful variations you could use. I like feta and dried fig or the Cypriot style pork and parsley. Once you have rolled a few you will get the knack. Vine leaves are magically good for you, they are amazing for your heart, have anti-inflammatory properties and are super-low in calories.

MAKES 10–12 *Ready in:* 1¼ hours

100ml olive oil
1 bunch spring onions, trimmed and finely
   chopped
1 bunch dill, finely chopped (stalks included)
200g sultanas

200g pine kernels
200g pudding rice
1 bunch fresh vine leaves (or use leaves in brine)
Juice of 1 lemon
Salt and freshly ground black pepper

Heat the olive oil then add the spring onions and dill. Cover and cook over a low heat for just a few minutes to allow the onions to sweat. Now add the sultanas and pine kernels. Give everything a good stir to coat with oil then add the rice and cook for a further minute or two until the grains become opaque. Take off the heat, season with a little salt and pepper.

Line a lightly oiled flameproof casserole dish with some vine leaves. Have the remaining leaves ready in a pile, vein side facing up. Place a leaf on a board, spoon on a teaspoon of the rice mixture, one third up from the centre base of the leaf. Now fold the leaf over the rice from the base then fold in the left and right side of the leaf before rolling up into a little cigar shape. Roll securely but not too tightly as the rice will swell up on cooking.

Place the rolled Yalaji snugly in the dish. Repeat until the base is full then continue another layer.

Place an inverted plate on top to weigh the Yalaji down. Pour cold water in and around to approx. 7cm above the vine leaves. Add the lemon juice.

Cover tightly and cook over a gentle heat for 45–50 minutes until nearly all the liquid has been absorbed and the vine leaves are tender. Either serve warm or leave to cool then chill before serving.

SOUPS, SALADS & VEGETABLES

Greeks usually have soup as a main meal so they tend to be hearty and filling. They are often served with green and black olives, with some bread on the side. I like to put a dollop of tahini sauce in or some Greek yogurt, and sprinkle with whatever fresh herbs I have to hand. If I am having soup at lunchtime it is great with a chunk of rye or wholemeal bread, but I like to keep it lighter for supper.

CHICKPEA AND CUMIN SOUP

SERVES 4 *Ready in:* 30 minutes

3 tsp cumin seeds
A pinch of dried chilli flakes
3 tbsp olive oil
1 red onion, chopped
900ml hot vegetable stock

2 x 400g can chopped tomatoes
400g can chickpeas, drained
Sea salt and freshly ground black pepper
2 tbsp natural Greek yogurt, to garnish
1 tbsp freshly chopped coriander

In a large saucepan dry fry the cumin seeds and chilli flakes, until the seeds start to jump around.

Add the oil and the onion, and gently cook until the onions become transparent but not browned. Season with a little black pepper.

Stir in the stock and tomatoes together with half of the chickpeas. Cover, bring to the boil then simmer for 20 minutes.

Blitz the soup to a smooth texture, adjust the seasoning and add the reserved chickpeas. Ladle into bowls, garnish with a swirl of yogurt and fresh coriander.

GREEK MINESTRONE SOUP

SERVES 4 *Ready in:* 1 hour

1 tbsp olive oil
2 rashers streaky bacon, chopped
1 clove garlic, chopped
1 red onion, finely chopped
1 large waxy potato, scrubbed and diced
2 carrots, chopped
2 sticks of celery, sliced
1 small leek, finely sliced
¼ tsp coriander seeds
1 bay leaf

400g can chopped tomatoes
1 medium courgette, chopped
400g can cannellini beans, rinsed and drained
900ml vegetable stock
75g orzo pasta (or small macaroni)
75g curly kale, stalks removed and chopped
2 tbsp freshly chopped coriander
5 tbsp grated kefalotiri cheese, optional (or use
    Emmenthal or Gruyère cheese)
Sea salt and freshly ground black pepper

Heat the oil in a large saucepan, add the bacon and cook until it starts to turn brown then add the garlic, onion, carrots, celery, leek, coriander seeds and bay leaf. Bring to the boil then simmer gently for 15 minutes, stirring occasionally.

Add the tomatoes, courgette, cannellini beans, and hot stock then cover and simmer for 20 minutes. Add the pasta and kale and simmer for a further 10 minutes or until the pasta is tender. Adjust the seasoning to taste.

Stir in the coriander then ladle into warmed bowls and sprinkle with the cheese.

SERVES 4–6 *Ready in:* 35 minutes

25g butter
3 tbsp olive oil
1 onion, finely sliced
3 cloves of garlic, chopped
900g parsnips, chopped

500g bulb fennel, chopped
1 tsp ground cumin
1 tsp ground turmeric
1.2 litres hot vegetable stock
Sea salt and freshly ground black pepper

Melt the butter and heat the olive oil in a large pan and gently cook the onion until softened but not coloured. Add the parsnips and fennel and continue to cook for 3–4 minutes.

Add the cumin and turmeric and coat the vegetables well, gently cooking for a further minute.

Add the stock, bring to a gentle boil then simmer for 15 minutes or until the vegetables are very tender.

Using a hand blender, blitz the soup until smooth. Season to taste then reheat gently to serve into warmed bowls.

LENTIL SOUP

Serve with green takistes olives, and crusty bread. I love spooning a dollop of hummus in the middle of this wonderful soup.

SERVES 6 *Ready in:* 1 hour

250g green lentils, rinsed
1 litre vegetable or chicken stock
1 large onion, finely chopped
4 cloves of garlic, chopped
2 carrots, sliced

1 stick of celery, sliced
400g can chopped tomatoes
150ml olive oil
1 tsp ground cumin
Sea salt and freshly ground black pepper

Place the rinsed lentils in a pan of cold water with a pinch of salt and bring to the boil for 2–3 minutes. Drain and return to the hot pan.

Add the stock and the remaining ingredients to the lentils, bring to the boil then cover and simmer for 30 minutes or until the lentils are soft but not splitting apart. Adjust the seasoning to taste. Serve.

TAHINI SOUP

SERVES 4–6 *Ready in:* 40 minutes

4 tbsp olive oil
2 onions, finely sliced
4 cloves of garlic, crushed
2 sweet potatoes, chopped
3 ripe tomatoes, skinned and coarsely chopped
   (or 200g canned chopped tomatoes)

1½ litres hot vegetable stock
100g orzo pasta (or small macaroni)
5 tbsp tahini
Juice of 1–2 lemons
Freshly chopped coriander
Sea salt and freshly ground black pepper

Heat the olive oil in a large pan and gently cook the onions until softened but not coloured. Add the garlic and remaining vegetables, cover and cook for 2–3 minutes.

Add the stock, bring to a gentle boil and simmer for 20 minutes or until the vegetables are very tender.

Using a hand blender, blitz the soup until smooth, sir in the pasta, cover and simmer for 10 minutes or until the pasta is tender, adding a drop more stock if the soup becomes too thick.

In a bowl, blend the tahini with the lemon juice, take a ladle of soup and mix in with the tahini then return the tahini mixture back to the soup, stirring well. Taste and sharpen with more lemon juice if required.

Serve into warmed bowls topped with freshly chopped coriander.

SERVES 4 *Ready in:* 50 minutes

5 tbsp olive oil
2 medium aubergines, cut into ¼ inch dice.
Salt
½ glass dry white wine
24 black Kalamata olives, pitted and chopped
3 tbsp capers, drained

3 cloves garlic crushed
2 tsp of lemon zest chopped
3 tbsp tomato puree
2 tsp of fresh oregano chopped (1 dry)
6 peppers different colours
1 cup water

Heat the oil in a large heavy bottomed pan, add the aubergine stir then salt and add wine. Cook for about 10 minutes till the aubergine is wilted.

Stir in the olives, garlic, capers, tomato paste oregano and zest.

Cook for about five minutes stirring.

Remove pan from heat and allow to cool slightly.

Slice the tops off the peppers, keep, then remove the seeds and core from the peppers.

Fill the peppers with the mixture and place the tops on top.

Pack closely together in a dish, pour the water around the peppers.

Preheat the oven to 200°C/fan 180°C/gas 6 and place the baking dish in the oven. Bake the peppers uncovered, until the shells are soft, for about 30 minutes.

Can be served hot or chilled.

This is such a staple Greek vegan dish. I like to make big batches and freeze it, getting some out when I want an extra dish for my meze platter. A wonderful accompaniment or wonderful on its own. My children like it when I sprinkle some feta cheese on top for the last few minutes of cooking, or even once out of the oven to add another depth to it.

SERVES 4 AS A MAIN *Ready in:* 1 hour

3 red onions, finely sliced
4 sun-dried tomatoes, sliced
1kg ripe tomatoes, peeled, seeded and chopped
4 cloves of garlic, chopped
3 celery stalks, finely sliced
2 large carrots, finely sliced
1 tbsp tomato puree

1 tsp sugar
1 tsp ground paprika
2 x 250g cans cannellini beans, rinsed
50g flat leaf parsley, chopped
50g dill, finely chopped
Salt and freshly ground black pepper

Preheat the oven to 180°C/fan 160°C/gas 4.

Heat the olive oil in a large flameproof casserole dish, add onions and cook gently for 5 minutes or until softened but not coloured. Add the remaining ingredients except for the herbs, mixing well. Season with some salt and pepper.

Cover and transfer to the oven to cook for 30 minutes. Stir in the herbs, add a little water or stock if the stew is drying out too much and continue to cook, uncovered for a further 10-15 minutes or until all the vegetables are tender. Serve piping hot on its own or as an accompaniment to grilled fish or meat.

OKRA STEW

I could live off this wonderful vegetable. I especially like eating it cold the day after it has been cooked. There is increasing evidence of okra having anti-diabetic properties, and many studies are now confirming okra as a potent blood glucose-lowering (or anti-diabetic) food. Add to that the amount of garlic in this dish and you really have a super healthy recipe.

SERVES 4 AS A MAIN *Ready in:* 45 minutes

500g fresh okra
120ml olive oil
2 onions, finely chopped
1 small bulb of garlic, peeled
500g fresh tomatoes, skinned and chopped (or

400g can chopped tomatoes)
½ tsp sugar
½ tsp ground cinnamon
1 large piece of cassia bark or cinnamon quill
3 tbsp red wine vinegar

Cut the stems off the okra, place in a bowl with a generous pinch of salt and the vinegar. Set aside for 20 minutes. Then wash and dry the okra.

Meanwhile heat the oil in a large pan, add onions and garlic and cook gently for 5 minutes or until softened but not coloured. Add the tomato, sugar, ground cinnamon and bark. Cover and simmer for 10 minutes. Season with some salt and pepper.

Gently fold in the okra, taking care not to break the pods. Cover and simmer for a further 15–20 minutes, adding a splash of water if it becomes too dry.

Serve at room temperature, or cold.

THE PERFECT TOMATO SAUCE

This really is the perfect tomato sauce for me, but if you like yours with a bit of cinnamon or extra black pepper, you should add it and make it perfect for you. This really is a recipe that it makes sense to make in large batches and freeze and the next time you want to make meatballs (*see* p.184) or a seafood stew (*see* p.146), half the work is already done. Though sometimes I just like to have it on its own on top of some wholemeal penne pasta and a dusting of kefalotiri cheese (a little parmesan will substitute).

SERVES 4 *Ready in:* 1 hour

4 tbsp olive oil
1 large onion, finely chopped
4 cloves of garlic, crushed
2 x 400g cans plum tomatoes
1 tsp sugar

1 tbsp red wine vinegar
3 stems of fresh basil
4 stems of fresh thyme
Extra-virgin olive oil, to serve
Sea salt and freshly ground black pepper

Heat the oil in a pan and cook the onion for 5 minutes or until softened but not coloured. Stir in the garlic and cook for another 2 minutes.

Tip in the tomatoes and crush to break up with a wooden spoon then add the sugar, vinegar and the thyme and basil stems, reserving the leaves. Season lightly.

Bring to a steady simmer, part-cover and simmer over a low heat for 30–40 minutes or until thick.

Adjust the seasoning, add the basil leaves, roughly torn, and drizzle in a little extra-virgin olive oil if you like, before serving.

THE PERFECT SALSA

SERVES 4 *Ready in:* 15 minutes

250g chopped tomatoes
1 green pepper, deseeded and diced
1 onion, diced
1 small bunch of fresh coriander, chopped
Zest and juice of 1 lime

1 small jalapeno pepper, chopped (include the
  seeds if you like the heat)
½ tsp ground cumin
½ tsp ground black pepper

Simply mix all the ingredients together and transfer to a serving bowl to serve.

SERVES 2 *Ready in:* 45 minutes

1 medium aubergine
2 tsp olive oil
Juice of ½ small lemon
100g couscous
300ml very hot vegetable stock
75g sultanas
4 sundried tomatoes in oil, drained and chopped
50g Kalamata olives, pitted and chopped
3 spring onions, finely sliced
25g pine nuts
¼ tsp ground cinnamon
Salt, to taste

DRESSING:
½ tsp saffron threads
4 heaped tbsp natural Greek yogurt
1 plump garlic clove, crushed
¼ tsp ground turmeric

Preheat the oven to 190°C/fan 170°C/gas 5. Place the saffron in a small dish and add 2 tbsp hot water, leaving to steep.

Leaving the stem on, cut the aubergine in half lengthways and score the flesh deeply in a criss-cross pattern using a sharp, pointed knife. Place in a shallow baking dish.

Mix the olive oil and the lemon juice and brush over the scored aubergine surface. Bake, uncovered, for 20–25 minutes.

Meanwhile place the couscous in a large bowl and pour on the stock. Leave to stand for 10 minutes for the couscous to absorb the stock. Fluff up with a fork, adding the sultanas, tomatoes, olives, spring onion and nuts. Sprinkle on the cinnamon and toss well together.

Remove the aubergine from the oven and when cool enough to handle, scoop out the flesh, taking care to keep the skins intact. Chop the flesh and mix into the couscous.

Place the aubergine skins back in the baking dish and fill each with the couscous, piling high. Scatter any remaining couscous around the edge of the dish. Return to the oven to heat through for 10 minutes.

Beat the dressing ingredients together, adding the remaining lemon juice. Serve the aubergine warm or cold accompanied with the saffron yogurt dressing.

BRAISED JERUSALEM ARTICHOKE WITH BROAD BEANS AND DILL

SERVES 6 *Ready in:* 40 minutes

12 medium sized Jerusalem artichokes
750g podded broad beans (or use frozen)
200ml olive oil
2 tbsp freshly chopped dill

Zest and juice of 2 lemons
1 tbsp plain flour
Sea salt and freshly ground black pepper

Clean, trim and wash the artichokes and cover in cold water with some of the lemon juice to prevent them discolouring. Drain when ready to use.

Place the oil in a heavy-based pan, add the broad beans and artichokes and cook for 2 minutes, coating the vegetables with the oil. Add the dill with 4 tbsp water and a little seasoning to taste. Cover and simmer for 20 minutes.

Blend the lemon juice with the flour and 5 minutes before the vegetables are cooked, blend in to the stew to thicken the pan juices. Sprinkle in the zest, remove from heat and serve.

ARTICHOKE CITY STYLE

SERVES 4–6 *Ready in:* 1 hour

10 small shallots
450g new potatoes eg Charlotte salad potatoes,
 halved
4 carrots, sliced
100ml olive oil
2 tbsp plain flour

Juice of 1 lemon
200ml vegetable stock
10 artichoke hearts, cut in half
6 spring onions, trimmed and chopped
50g freshly chopped dill
Sea salt and freshly ground black pepper

Heat half the olive oil in a large flameproof casserole dish. Add the shallots, potatoes and carrots and cook for 5 minutes.

Sprinkle in the flour, cook for 1 minute then blend in the lemon juice, stock and remaining oil. Cover and bring to the boil then reduce the heat to simmer for 15–20 minutes or until the potatoes are just 'al dente'. Do check and add a drop more liquid if required.

Add the artichokes, spring onions and fresh dill and season with salt and pepper. Cover and simmer for a further 15 minutes or until the artichokes are tender.

GARLIC, MINT AND TOMATO CASSOULET

....

SERVES 2 AS A MAIN, 4 AS AN ACCOMPANIMENT *Ready in:* 25 minutes

1 tbsp olive oil
1 small red onion, chopped
2 cloves of garlic, chopped
200g can chopped tomatoes

200g canned butter beans, drained
200g frozen or fresh podded broad beans
1 tbsp freshly chopped mint
Sea salt and freshly ground black pepper

Heat half the olive oil in a pan and add the onion and garlic and cook gently to soften but not colour.

Add the tomatoes and simmer to reduce a little for 2–3 minutes then stir in the beans.

Simmer, part covered, for 5 minutes to cook the broad beans and thicken the sauce.

Season with salt and pepper. Sprinkle with mint before serving.

CUMIN POTATOES

....

Cyprus potatoes are grown in distinctive clay soil, which makes them very nutritious and exceptionally tasty; there is no better potato in the world. You can find them in Greek, Mediterranean, Asia or Middle-Eastern delis, and larger supermarkets are now stocking them too.

SERVES 4 *Ready in:* 90 minutes

6 medium Cypriot potatoes, halved lengthways
1 large onion, sliced into rings
2 tsp ground cumin
2 tsp ground cinnamon

2 tbsp extra-virgin olive oil
400g can plum tomatoes
Sea salt and freshly ground black pepper

Place the potatoes and onions in a large shallow roasting dish.

Sprinkle on the cumin, cinnamon, salt and pepper, to taste and then drizzle with the oil. Toss together well.

Use your hands to crush the tomatoes over the potatoes. Pour 200ml water into the base of the tin.

Cover with foil and cook for 40 minutes, then remove the foil and reduce the oven temperature to 180°C/fan 160°C/gas 4 for another 20–30 minutes or until the potatoes are tender.

Cumin is such a wonderful spice. It is part of the parsley family and has a wonderful aromatic flavour. Not only does it taste delicious but it has super healing qualities; it is protective against memory loss and the damaging effects of stress on the body; it has anti-asthmatic properties; it is effective in increasing insulin sensitivity and actually found more effective at reducing blood glucose than some anti-diabetic drugs.

Growing your own herbs and vegetables is a lovely thing to do, even if all you have is a small window box. Plant some mint and rosemary; these are hardy herbs and will survive a little neglect. The other thing to grow is peas as they just keep on giving. My wonderful friend Gina planted peas for me in April and we had peas all summer. I harvested the last of the pea shoots in early March and even with the somewhat watery English summer, they still tasted amazing.

SERVES 4 *Ready in:* 20 minutes

250g brown rice
2 courgettes, sliced thinly, lengthways
1 tbsp zaatar
150g fresh garden peas
Zest and juice of 1 lemon

1 tbsp harissa paste
25g fresh mint, leaves stripped
50g pea shoots
Sea salt and freshly ground black pepper

Cook the rice according to pack instructions. Leave to cool.

Meanwhile heat a griddle or barbecue. Brush the courgettes with oil, sprinkle over the zaatar and cook in batches for 2 minutes on each side until just tender and seared. Remove from heat and set aside.

Tip the peas into a pan of boiling water, cook for 3 minutes then drain and set aside.

Make the dressing in a large bowl by whisking together the lemon zest and juice, the harissa and olive oil. Add the rice and toss to coat.

Gently fold in the courgettes, peas, mint leaves and pea shoots. Season and serve immediately.

SPINACH RICE WITH DILL AND LEMON

SERVES 4 *Ready in:* 25 minutes

200ml Greek extra-virgin olive oil
1 large onion, finely chopped
1kg tender young spinach, washed and chopped
100g fresh dill, finely chopped

250g long grain brown rice
Juice of 2 lemons
Sea salt and freshly ground black pepper

Start by heating the oil in a large pan then cook the onions until softened but not coloured. Add the spinach, two thirds of the dill and 500ml hot water. Stir and bring to a steady boil.

Stir in the rice, season with a little salt, reduce the heat and cover, simmering until the rice has cooked and all the water has been absorbed.

Just before serving, stir in the remaining dill, season with black pepper and squeeze over the lemon juice.

TABBOULEH

SERVES 4 *Ready in:* 20 minutes

175g bulgur wheat
3 tomatoes, diced
2 chopped spring onions
½ cucumber, peeled and diced
1 tbsp freshly chopped parsley

FOR THE DRESSING:
1 tbsp olive oil
1 tbsp lemon juice
Sea salt and freshly ground black pepper

Cook the bulgur wheat according to the pack instructions then drain.

Now simply mix with the tomato, spring onions, cucumber and parsley.

Make the dressing by mixing the olive oil and lemon juice together, seasoning well. Pour over the bulgur wheat and mix through.

Serve cool but not chilled.

POURGOURI OR CRACKED WHEAT WITH TOMATOES AND ONION

Pourgouri or cracked wheat is something that is eaten often in the Greek diet. Sometimes we eat it as a main meal on its own served with some black olives, Greek yogurt and half a red onion, other times it is used as an accompaniment for Stifado (see p.184). Here I have shown you how to make tomato pougouri but there are many variations, all so easy to make and very tasty. White pourgouri is without the tomatoes which is good with stews. You can also make it up and add pine kernels and sultanas.

SERVES 4 *Ready in:* 20 minutes

2 tbsp olive oil
1 large onion, chopped
1 heaped tsp of cinnamon
1 nest vermicelli or angel hair pasta

250g cracked wheat or pourgouri
2 x 400g cans chopped tomatoes
Sea salt and freshly ground black pepper

Heat the oil in a pan. Gently cook the onion until softened and golden. Crush the vermicelli or pasta in your hand and scatter onto the onions, adding a pinch of salt and pepper. Stir in the tomatoes.

Sprinkle in the cracked wheat, stir well then add 400ml boiled hot water. Continue stirring until all the water has been absorbed – this only takes a minute or two. Adjust the seasoning.

Now turn off the heat, cover the pan with a clean tea towel and leave to stand for 10 minutes to allow the cracked wheat to continue steaming to perfection.

CHICKPEA AND FETA SALAD

Also know as *Garbanzos,* we Greeks use a lot of chickpeas, they are the main ingredient of hummus and feature prominently during the vegan fasting of the Greek religious calendar. Chickpeas are jam-packed with fibre and excellent vegan and gluten-free protein. They are high in iron which will give an energy boost and are also wonderful for good hair, skin and nails. I love them roasted as a snack. Take a can of chickpeas, rinse them well, dry them and discard any skins. Drizzle them with olive oil and mix them well and put them on a baking tray in the oven on 180°C/fan 160°C/gas 4 for 20–30 minutes, take them out and season as you please. I like sea salt, chilli and cumin.

SERVES 4 *Ready in:* 20 minutes

1 small red onion, finely sliced
1 fresh red chilli, deseeded and finely sliced
250g cherry tomatoes
Juice of 1 lime
3 tbsp olive oil

400g can chickpeas, drained and rinsed
3 tbsp freshly chopped mint
3 tbsp freshly chopped coriander
100g feta cheese
Sea salt and freshly ground black pepper, to taste

Place the onion and chilli, half the lime juice and the olive oil in a large bowl. Season with a little salt and pepper.

Heat the chickpeas in a non-stick pan then add all but a small handful to the onion mixture. Mash the remaining handful and add to the bowl.

Leave the chickpeas to marinade a little, then mix in the chopped herbs. Add a little more lime juice if required. Spoon onto a serving plate and crumble on the feta cheese.

Anyone that knows me knows that I add **cinnamon** to EVERYTHING! Savoury or sweet I think it always benefits from a teaspoon of cinnamon. I have not put it in to every recipe, but I wanted to! Cinnamon for me takes me back to being a child; warm and aromatic, it transports me back to the long summers we would have as children in Greece and Cyprus. It is the most beneficial spice of all, it is loaded with antioxidants, has anti-inflammatory properties, it can cut the risk of heart disease, it improves sensitivity to insulin so lowers blood sugar levels and has a powerful anti-diabetic effect. All that and it tastes amazing!

SERVES 4 *Ready in:* 40 minutes

4 tbsp olive oil
400g butternut squash, cut into 2cm lengths
2 sweet potatoes, scrubbed and cut into 2cm
  lengths
2 cloves garlic, finely sliced
1 tsp cumin seeds
½ tsp ground turmeric

100g lentils
2 bay leaves
1 tbsp red wine vinegar
1 large red onion, thinly sliced
30g walnut pieces
2 tbsp freshly chopped mint leaves
Sea salt and freshly ground black pepper, to taste

Preheat the oven to 200°C/fan 180°C/gas 6. In a large bowl, mix together the oil, squash, potatoes, garlic and spices making sure they are well coated.

Spread onto a lightly oiled baking tray and bake for 20–25 minutes or until nicely coloured.

Meanwhile place the lentils in a pan with the bay leaves and enough water to cover well. Bring to the boil then simmer for 15–20 minutes or until tender. Drain well, discarding the bay leaves.

Place all the remaining ingredients in a large bowl and add the warm roasted vegetables and lentils. Toss gently. Serve.

WARM CYPRUS POTATO SALAD

....

SERVES 4 *Ready in:* 30 minutes

4 large Cypriot potatoes, scrubbed and diced
3 tbsp extra-virgin olive oil
1 large onion, thinly sliced
3 cloves garlic, chopped
1 tsp ground cumin
1 tsp ground cinnamon

400g can chopped tomatoes
250g baby spinach leaves, washed
4 tbsp freshly chopped coriander
2 tbsp red wine vinegar
100g feta cheese
Sea salt and freshly ground black pepper, to taste

Cook the potatoes in boiling water for 4–5 minutes or until just tender. Drain. Heat the olive oil in a pan and gently fry the potatoes until golden. Remove and set aside.

Now add the onion, garlic and spices. Cook until the onions have softened but not coloured. Return the potatoes to the pan with the tomatoes. Increase the heat to a steady simmer for 4–5 minutes.

Remove from the heat, stir in the spinach, coriander and vinegar, mixing well to wilt the spinach in the residual heat. Add the cheese and let it sit for a minute or two before spooning straight from the pan.

WATERMELON AND HALLOUMI SALAD

....

SERVES 2 *Ready in:* 10 minutes

750g chilled watermelon, cut into chunks
175g halloumi, grated

A handful of freshly torn mint leaves

Divide the watermelon between two plates, scatter on the cheese and finish with a sprinkling of mint. Enjoy.

WATERMELON, FETA AND OLIVE SALAD

....

SERVES 2 *Ready in:* 10 minutes

750g grilled watermelon, cut into chunks
75g feta cheese
10 olives

2 tsp lemon juice
2 tsp olive oil

Arrange the watermelon in 2 bowls, crumble on the feta cheese and scatter on the olives. Drizzle with a little fresh lemon juice and olive oil. Serve with a grinding of fresh black pepper.

COUSCOUS AND POMEGRANATE SALAD

This is vitality in a salad. Full of fibre and fresh flavours and so easy to make it is a regular at my table. It also looks beautiful. If you are serving when pomegranates are not in season you could substitute them for dried cranberries. Use whatever herbs you have at home. I like to add fresh pea shoots and a teaspoon of cinnamon too to give some variation. Pomegranate syrup gives that little bit of zing too.

SERVES 4–6 *Ready in:* 30 minutes

400g couscous
400ml hot vegetable stock
100g flaked almonds
400g can chick peas, rinsed and drained
½ tsp ground coriander
Zest and juice of 1 lime

3 tbsp freshly chopped mint
3 tbsp freshly chopped coriander
Seeds from 2 pomegranates
A drizzle of extra-virgin olive oil
A drizzle of pomegranate syrup
Sea salt and freshly ground black pepper, to taste

Put the couscous in a large bowl and pour on 400ml stock. Cover the bowl with a plate and allow to stand for 5 minutes for the couscous to absorb the stock. Fluff up with a fork.

Meanwhile heat a large non-stick frying pan and cook the almonds until nicely browned and tasty. Remove to absorbent kitchen paper to cool.

Add 1 tbsp oil to the pan, warm through, then add the chickpeas and ground coriander. Season with a little salt and pepper and fry for 3–4 minutes, tossing around the pan until they become crispy. Add the lime juice and cook for another minute before adding the couscous.

Stir in the flaked almonds, the pomegranate seeds, chopped mint and coriander and the lime zest. Stir to combine, finishing with a good drizzle of olive oil. Serve.

SERVES 4–6 *Ready in:* 30 minutes

4 tbsp olive oil
1 onion, finely chopped
300g bulgur wheat
1 red chilli
150g baby spinach leaves
4 spring onions
30g fresh coriander

Zest and juice of 1 lime
2 red peppers, deseeded and sliced
2 peaches, sliced
1 ripe avocado, stoned and cut into chunks
100g feta, crumbled
Lime wedges, to garnish

Heat 1 tbsp oil in a pan and cook the onion until softened but not coloured. Add the bulgur wheat and pour on 600ml hot water. Bring to the boil then reduce the heat to a low simmer for 20 minutes. Remove from the heat and set aside.

Meanwhile place the chilli, spinach, spring onion, coriander stalks and leaves (holding back a handful of leaves to garnish) into a food processor with 2 tbsp olive oil and the zest of 1 lime. Blitz to a salsa (or finely chop by hand). Stir into the bulgur wheat.

On a preheated griddle, cook the peppers and peaches for 5–6 minutes until lightly charred and softened.

Arrange the bulgur wheat onto plates and scatter the griddled peach and peppers on top. Add the avocado and feta. Drizzle on a little oil and serve garnished with a lime wedge.

ANCHOVY, QUAILS EGG AND ASPARAGUS SALAD

This is not really a recipe, but I wanted to show how easy it is to throw together some fresh and nutritious flavours and have a wonderful meal. If you don't have quinoa, use couscous or brown rice; if you don't have asparagus use some cooked steamed broccoli, and with a few anchovies you can always make a delicious salad. Serve with some toasted rye bread that has a drizzle of olive oil and a crushed clove of garlic on it.

SERVES 1 *Ready in:* 10 minutes

50g pre-cooked quinoa
50g spring greens, shredded
1 asparagus spear, shaved into ribbons with
   potato peeler
3–4 hard-boiled quails eggs
50g anchovies
1 tsp freshly snipped chives

FOR THE DRESSING:
1 tbsp extra-virgin olive oil
1 tbsp cider vinegar
A pinch of salt and freshly ground black pepper

Assemble all the ingredients on a plate.

Beat together the ingredients for the dressing and season well. Drizzle over the salad. Serve at room temperature.

SERVES 6 *Ready in:* 30 minutes

4 small cooked beetroot, cut into 2cm dice
Juice of 1 small lemon
6 tbsp extra-virgin olive oil, or to taste
Coarse-grain sea salt and cracked black pepper
   to taste
3 large navel oranges

1 large bunch watercress, sprigs only
225g feta cheese, drained, cut into 1cm dice
12 green and black Greek olives, drained
2 tsp dried *rigani*, (wild oregano, or if freshly
   chopped use 2 tbsp)

Combine the beetroot, most of the lemon juice, 2 tbsp olive oil, salt and pepper in a glass bowl. Cover and set aside.

Peel the oranges, cutting away any white pith with a small, sharp knife. Cut the orange crossways into 2cm slices. Remove the pithy centres with the point of a knife. Arrange the slices on a plate, tightly cover, and refrigerate until chilled.

When ready to serve, line the edges of a chilled serving platter with the watercress then arrange the orange slices in a single overlapping layer on the inside edge of this border. Make a circle of the beetroot inside the oranges; drizzle its marinade over. Finally scatter the feta in the centre.

Sprinkle the oranges with a little salt, the beetroot and feta with the *rigani* and olives. Sprinkle the remaining lemon juice, olive oil and some pepper over the salad then enjoy!

SERVES 4 *Ready in:* 30 minutes

2 aubergines
3 peppers, red or green, sliced thickly
1 large onion, chopped
1 small chilli
2 cloves garlic, minced
2 large tomatoes, chopped or 200g can chopped
  tomatoes

100ml olive oil
175g feta cheese, cubed
3 tbsp freshly chopped parsley
Sea salt and freshly ground black pepper

Slice the aubergines thickly and place them in a bowl of cold water with some salt. Leave to soak.

Meanwhile prepare the tomato sauce. Heat 2 tbsp oil in a shallow ovenproof dish and cook the onion for 4–5 minutes until softened but not coloured. Add the garlic, whole chilli and tomato and simmer for 5 minutes.

Meanwhile squeeze the water out of the aubergines and dry them on absorbent kitchen paper.

Heat the remaining oil in a frying pan and sauté the aubergine slices in batches, so they brown on both sides.

Transfer the aubergines to the pan with the tomato sauce and arrange in a layer.

Now fry the peppers in the olive oil and when lightly browned add to the aubergines.

Spoon the tomato sauce around the aubergine and peppers to coat, then dot the cubes of feta in amongst the dish.

Transfer to a preheated oven 170°C/fan 150°C/gas 3 and bake for 20 minutes. Sprinkle with the parsley and serve.

I have got into the habit of regularly roasting butternut squash and keeping it in the fridge as it is such a wonderful addition to any salad and tastes great hot or cold. Butternut squash is rich in vitamin A which helps us have lovely skin and hair, it is also rich in phytonutrients and antioxidants. If you wanted to make this salad a little lighter you could leave out the pasta.

SERVES 4 *Ready in:* 40 minutes

1 tbsp runny honey
4 tbsp olive oil
½ tsp dried red chilli flakes
800g butternut squash, chopped
400g whole wheat penne pasta

3 garlic cloves, very thinly sliced
30g fresh thyme
175g feta cheese, crumbled (optional)
Sea salt and freshly ground black pepper

Preheat the oven to 200°C/fan 180°C/gas 6. Mix the honey with half the oil and the chilli. Put the squash on a baking tray lined with non-stick paper, season and drizzle with the honey mix. Roast for 20-25 minutes or until tender and golden.

Meanwhile cook the pasta in a large pan of boiling water according to the pack instructions. Drain when tender and return to the pan.

Heat the remaining olive oil in a frying pan. Add the garlic and thyme sprigs and cook, stirring, for 2 minutes or until the garlic is softened but not coloured too much.

Toss the squash, thyme and half the feta into the hot pasta. Season and top with the remaining feta.

SERVES 4 *Ready in:* 30 minutes

3 heads of fennel
4 tbsp olive oil
350g whole wheat penne pasta
225g Greek black olives, pitted and sliced

Finely grated zest and juice of 1 lemon
200g kasseri or taleggio cheese, sliced
½ tsp dried oregano
Sea salt and freshly ground black pepper

Preheat the grill to medium. Cut the fennel into quarters lengthways, discarding any outer leaves then cut away the core and thinly slice lengthways.

Heat 2 tbsp oil in a large frying pan, add the fennel with a little seasoning and cook for 8–10 minutes or until golden and tender.

Meanwhile cook the pasta in a large pan of boiling water according to the pack instructions. Drain when tender and return to the pan. Stir in the fennel, olives and lemon zest, folding together well.

Tip the mixture into a large, shallow ovenproof dish and drizzle with the remaining olive oil and lemon juice.

Lay the cheese slices on top and sprinkle with a little oregano.

Cook under the grill for 5 minutes or until the cheese has melted and is beginning to turn golden. Serve immediately.

FISH, MEAT & POULTRY

BABY CUTTLEFISH

This recipe works equally well with squid or octopus too, all of which are high in protein and low in fat. It also has more of an oriental slant and you can add your favourite flavours to cuttlefish as it does not have a strong flavour of its own, but takes on the flavour of whatever you have marinated it with.

SERVES 4 *Ready in:* 10 minutes plus 2 hours marinating

500g baby cuttle fish
100ml light soy sauce
1 tsp oyster sauce
1 tbsp brown sugar
½ small red chilli, chopped
1 tbsp freshly grated root ginger

2 tbsp toasted sesame seeds
Zest and juice of ½ small orange
1 tbsp olive oil plus extra for brushing
Sea salt and freshly ground black pepper, to
  season

Place the cuttle fish in a bowl. Mix together all the other ingredients to make a marinade and pour over the fish, coating them well. Cover and leave for a minimum of 2 hours, ideally overnight in the fridge.

Cook the cuttle fish over a barbecue or in a griddle pan for 2–3 minutes, brushing the fish with some marinade and a little extra oil. Take care not to overcook.

Serve warm as part of a meze.

Whenever I am in Greece or Cyprus I love seeing a row of octopuses drying on the line. My dad is a great octopus fisher and we always have a competition to see who will catch most. So far I think I am winning! When I was a child we would always see the fishermen bashing the octopus against the rocks to tenderise them before cooking but now there is a much easier way – 48 hours in the freezer. Once they are out they are wonderfully tender and ready to cook. So it makes sense to always buy frozen octopus.

SERVES 4 AS PART OF A MEZE *Ready in:* 2½ hours

1 whole octopus, cleaned
Sprigs of fresh rosemary
Extra-virgin olive oil

Juice of 2 lemons
A handful of flat leaf parsley, chopped
Salt, to taste

Preheat the oven to 150°C/fan 120°C/Gas 2. Wash and clean the octopus, rinsing thoroughly. Lay the octopus in a large, shallow roasting dish. Drizzle generously with olive oil and tuck the rosemary sprigs in amongst the octopus.

Roast for 2–2½ hours or until tender. Transfer to a plate and using scissors snip the flesh into bite size pieces.

Whisk up a dressing of olive oil and lemon juice (approx. 2/1 ratio of oil to juice); it will turn into a smooth emulsion. Season to taste with salt then stir in the parsley. Drizzle the dressing over the warm octopus.

Serve warm or at room temperature.

FRESHLY COOKED MUSSELS WITH GARLICKY TOMATOES

All the effort for this recipe goes into cleaning the mussels. Once that is done, it is quick and easy, and needs to be eaten straight away whilst hot. I also like to eat mussels cooked with parsley and retsina wine; it transports me right back to island-hopping as a student.

SERVES 4 AS PART OF A MEZE *Ready in:* 25 minutes

1 kg bag fresh rope-grown mussels
4 tbsp olive oil
4 plump cloves of garlic, crushed
3 tbsp sun-dried tomatoes puree

450g vine tomatoes, chopped
1 tsp fresh lemon thyme leaves, roughly chopped
Crusty bread, for serving
Salt and freshly ground black pepper

Wash the mussels in a colander under running water, scraping off any barnacles. Pull away the beards and discard any broken shells. Tap any open mussels against the side of the sink and discard those that do not close immediately.

Warm the oil in a large saucepan and fry the garlic for 30 seconds. Add the tomato puree and 4 tbsp cold water.

Add the chopped tomatoes and half the thyme to the pan with plenty of black pepper and a little salt. Bring to the boil and cook for a few minutes until the tomatoes have softened slightly.

Add the mussels, cover with a lid and cook for 5 minutes, shaking the pan frequently, until the mussels have opened – discard any that remain closed.

Serve in shallow serving bowls, topping with the remaining thyme and a side serving of crusty bread.

Fresh sardines are seriously the best fish you can eat, rich in vitamin D which promotes bone health and prevents some forms of cancer and packed with protein. When you are buying your sardines look for ones that smell fresh, are firm to the touch and have bright eyes and skin – that way you will ensure you are getting the freshest.

Mackerel is another fish like sardines that is so good for you and so very reasonable to buy. It is full of omega-3 fatty acids which are anti-carcinogenic and also play a major role in keeping our brains young and healthy. Mackerel cooked this way also goes well with pourgouri (*see* p.99) or on top of warm Cyprus potato salad (*see* p.104).

This dish is nice eaten with a tomato and onion salad and extra lemon wedges for squeezing. Mop up the juices with crusty bread.

SERVES 4–6 *Ready in:* 40 minutes

12 large fresh sardines, cleaned and gutted
2 lemons
5 tbsp extra-virgin olive oil

4 tbsp freshly chopped oregano (or 1 tbsp dried)
Sea salt and freshly ground black pepper
Lemon wedges, for squeezing

Preheat the oven to 180°C/fan 160°C/gas 4. Arrange the sardines in a single layer on a baking tray.

Thinly slice 1 lemon and arrange over and around the fish. Squeeze the juice from the second lemon over the sardines.

Scatter on the oregano, drizzle with olive oil and season lightly.

Bake for 20–30 minutes or until the fish is tender. Serve from the tray with lemon wedges for squeezing.

SERVES 4 *Ready in:* 30 minutes

4 mackerel, filleted
400g tender spinach leaves

FOR THE DRESSING:
1 tsp fennel seeds
1 tsp coriander seeds
6 tbsp olive oil

1 clove of garlic, crushed
2 shallots, finely diced
Zest of 1 lemon
2 tomatoes, peeled, deseeded and diced
1 tbsp freshly chopped coriander
2 tsp white wine vinegar
Sea salt and freshly ground black pepper

Heat the fennel and coriander seeds in a small frying pan until they become aromatic and toasty. Add 2 tbsp olive oil and the garlic and leave to infuse for 10–20 minutes.

In another small pan cook the shallots in 2 tbsp olive oil until softened. Add the lemon zest, chopped herbs, the infused seeds and garlic, chopped tomato and the vinegar. Warm through gently for 4–5 minutes. Season with a little salt and pepper.

Meanwhile preheat the grill to medium-high. Season the mackerel fillets and place on a lightly oiled tray, skin side up. Grill for 3–4 minutes or until cooked and the skin crisp.

Heat the remaining oil in a wok or pan and add the spinach. Cook over a high heat for 1–2 minutes to wilt the leaves. Season.

Divide the spinach between 4 warmed plates and top with the mackerel. Drizzle the coriander sauce over each and serve immediately.

GRIDDLED HERRING AND NUTMEG MASH

SERVES 2 *Ready in:* 30 minutes, plus 1 hour marinating

2 herring, filleted
2 tbsp olive oil
Juice of ½ lemon
1 tsp ground coriander
1 clove of garlic, crushed

500g potatoes, cut into chunks
2–3 tbsp natural Greek yogurt
½ tsp ground nutmeg
Fresh coriander sprigs
Sea salt and freshly ground black pepper

Lay the herring in a dish with the olive oil, lemon juice, ground coriander, garlic and a little salt and pepper. Cover and leave to marinate for 1 hour.

Meanwhile cook the potatoes in plenty of boiling water until tender. Drain and mash with the yogurt. Season and beat in the nutmeg. Keep warm.

Meanwhile preheat the grill to medium-high. Drain the herring and place on a baking tray, skin side up. Grill for 2–3 minutes on each side or until cooked through.

Spoon the mashed potato onto warmed plates and top with the herring and fresh coriander to garnish.

HERBY SEA BREAM

SERVES 4 *Ready in:* 30 minutes, plus 1 hour marinating

4 whole sea bream, gutted and cleaned
3 tbsp olive oil
Zest and juice of 1 lemon
3 cloves of garlic
2 bay leaves

2 tbsp freshly chopped flat leaf parsley
2 tbsp freshly chopped oregano
1 tbsp freshly chopped thyme leaves
½ tsp dried chilli flakes
Seas salt and freshly ground black pepper

Score the skin of the sea bream and insert deep slits diagonally on each side of the fish. Season with salt and black pepper.

Place all the remaining ingredients in a large shallow dish, mix together then add the fish, coating well. Cover and leave in a cool place to marinade, ideally in the fridge overnight.

Bring the fish to room temperature, drain from the marinade, then place under a medium grill or on the barbecue for around 10–12 minutes on each side or bake in a preheated oven at 180°C/fan 160°C/gas 4 for 25 minutes, covering with foil for the first 10 minutes.

Serve with the marinade drizzled over, a splash of olive oil and an extra squeeze of lemon juice (optional).

TROUT FILLETS WRAPPED IN HIROMERI SERVED WITH LENTILS

Whenever I travel to Cyprus I go up to the village of Agros in the mountains as they are renowned there for producing wonderful cured meats like hiromeri and lounza. These are cured in the old-fashioned way with no nitrates. If you have a Greek deli near you, make sure that you buy naturally cured meats. Wrapping the trout in this wonderful salty cured ham works so well.

SERVES 4 *Ready in:* 60 minutes

225g lentils
4 trout, filleted
5 tbsp olive oil
8 sprigs fresh thyme
8 slices hiromeri or Parma ham

25g fresh dill, chopped
25g fresh flat leaf parsley, chopped
Juice of 1 lemon
Salt and freshly ground black pepper

Preheat the oven to 220°C/fan 200°C/gas 8.

Place the lentils in a saucepan, cover with cold water and slowly bring to the boil and simmer for 15 minutes or until tender.

On a board, place 2 trout fillets skin side down. Season with salt and pepper and drizzle with a little oil. Place 2 sprigs of thyme in the middle, sandwich the fillets back together and wrap with 2 slices of the hiromeri or Parma ham. Place on an oiled baking tray. Repeat with the remaining 3 trout.

Roast the trout for 10–12 minutes or until tender.

Meanwhile make the dressing for the lentils; whisk the lemon juice and 4 tbsp olive oil. Season to taste.

Drain the lentils thoroughly, return to the warm pan then stir in the dressing and chopped herbs.

Spoon the lentils onto warmed plates with the trout and serve.

SERVES 4 *Ready in:* 60 minutes

1kg fresh fish eg sea bream, sea bass, John Dory,
  halibut, cod or haddock
3 tbsp olive oil
1 large lemon
1 large onion, sliced
2–3 plump garlic cloves, crushed

1 x 400g can chopped tomatoes
2 tbsp chopped parsley
1 tsp fennel seeds or crushed coriander seeds
½ glass (100ml) retsina
Salt and freshly ground black pepper

Preheat the oven to 190˚C/fan 170˚C/gas 5.

Scale and clean the fish; place whole to just fit in an oiled baking or roasting dish. Sprinkle generously with salt, freshly ground pepper and the juice from half the lemon.

Heat the remaining oil in a saucepan, fry the onion and crushed garlic over a medium heat until the onion is soft and transparent, taking care not to burn the garlic. Now stir in the tomatoes, parsley, crushed seeds and retsina. Cook the sauce for a few minutes then season with salt and pepper.

Pour the sauce over the fish. Cut the remaining lemon into thin slices and arrange on top of the fish. Cover the dish with foil and bake in the centre of the oven for about 40–45 min.

SERVES 2 *Ready in:* 30 minutes

2 bay leaves
½ tbsp fresh rosemary leaves, stripped from the stem
3 tbsp extra-virgin olive oil

2 cloves of garlic, finely sliced
1 large lemon, sliced into 8
Sea salt and freshly ground black pepper

Preheat the oven to 200°C/fan 180°C/gas 6.

Wash the fish well, sprinkle with salt and leave to drain. Rinse again and dry with kitchen paper.

Have ready 2 sheets of kitchen parchment paper large enough to parcel up each fish. Place 1 bay leaf in the middle of each sheet. Season the 2 fish with salt and pepper and then sprinkle the rosemary, garlic and a drizzle of olive oil into the cavity and over the skin.

Stack each fish on a bay leaf, divide the lemon slices over the top then bring the paper together, carefully folding over and tucking in the ends to form a tight seal, yet still leaving room for the steam to waft around the fish. Transfer to a baking tray.

Place in the oven and cook for 20 minutes. Slide the parcels onto warmed plates and serve, allowing your guest the pleasure of tearing open their parcel, homing in on the wonderful aroma and treat in store.

RED MULLET WITH ROSE PETALS

SERVES 4 AS A STARTER, 2 AS A MAIN COURSE *Ready in:* 20 minutes

4 red mullet, scaled and gutted
2 tbsp olive oil
6 sprigs of fresh rosemary
1 tsp pink peppercorns

450ml rosé wine
Pink garden rose petals, to garnish
Sea salt and freshly ground black pepper

Heat the oil in a pan large enough to take the whole fish in a single layer. Season the fish with salt and pepper and place in the pan with the rosemary and pink peppercorns. Cook in the hot oil for 4 minutes.

Gently turn the fish and cook on the other side for 4 minutes.

Add the wine and simmer for 2–3 minutes. Remove the pan from the heat and then add the rose petals. Serve.

RED MULLET WITH CORIANDER AND SAFFRON

SERVES 2 *Ready in:* 15 minutes

3 tbsp extra-virgin olive oil
1 tbsp coriander seeds, crushed
1 tbsp lemon juice
2 red mullet, filleted and scaled
1 tbsp plain flour

1 tbsp. natural Greek yogurt
1 pinch saffron threads
A handful of salad leaves, to garnish
Sea salt and freshly ground black pepper

Gently heat 2 tbsp oil in a small pan and add the crushed coriander seeds. Cook for 2 minutes, but do not brown the seeds else they will become bitter tasting.

Add the lemon juice, remove from heat, and stir in the yogurt and saffron.

Dust the red mullet with the flour. Heat 1 tbsp oil in a non-stick frying pan and cook the fillets for 2 minutes on each side.

To serve, place one fillet on each warmed plate, spoon some of the yogurt mixture over and top with the second fillet. Pile some salad leaves on the fish and serve.

BAKED SALMON WITH THYME AND LEMON OAT CRUST

SERVES 4 *Ready in:* 35 minutes

4 salmon fillets
50g porridge oats
Grated zest of ½ lemon
1 tbsp freshly chopped thyme

35g pine nuts, chopped
1 egg, beaten
1 tbsp olive oil
Sea salt and freshly ground black pepper

Preheat the oven to 200°C/fan 180°C/gas 6. Place the salmon skin side down on a baking sheet.

Mix together the oats, lemon zest, thyme, pine nuts and seasoning. Add the egg to bind the ingredients together.

Brush the salmon fillets with a little oil then pat on an oat crust to cover the fillet surface. Drizzle with any remaining oil.

Bake for 20 minutes or until the salmon is cooked crisp and golden through the crust.

BAKED MACKEREL WITH TOMATO SAUCE, CAPERS AND OLIVES

SERVES 4 *Ready in:* 20 minutes

1 quantity of perfect tomato sauce (*see* p.89)
250g fine green beans, trimmed
4 fresh mackerel, filleted, skin on

2 tbsp olive oil
Sea salt and freshly ground black pepper, to season

In a large pan, cook the beans in lightly salted water for 2 minutes until very al dente, drain in a colander and refresh in cold water. Drain.

Preheat the oven to 210°C/fan 190°C/gas 7.

Using a sharp-tipped knife, slash diagonal slits in the mackerel skin at 3cm intervals. Brush the fillets with a little oil and season. Heat a large non-stick frying pan and in batches, sear the skin-side of the mackerel fillets for 1 minute or until lightly golden, seasoning the underside whilst they are cooking.

Combine the green beans and tomato sauce in an ovenproof oblong dish. Nestle the mackerel fillets in the sauce and place the dish in the oven. Roast for 10–15 minutes or until cooked through.

SPICED COD WITH CHICKPEA MASH

This recipe is super-easy and it tastes super-wonderful. The spices with the chickpeas and spinach just perfect this dish. If you want you can use any other firm white fish instead of cod.

SERVES 2 *Ready in:* 35 minutes

2 x 175g cod fillets
4 tbsp natural Greek yogurt
½ tsp ground coriander
½ tsp ground cumin
½ tsp ground turmeric

FOR THE MASH
2 tbsp olive oil
A pinch of dried red chilli flakes
2 cloves of garlic, crushed
Zest and juice of 1 lemon
400g can chickpeas, rinsed and drained
50g baby spinach leaves
Sea salt and freshly ground black pepper

Wipe the fish and place on a clean plate. Mix half the yogurt and spices together, season with a little salt then coat the fish completely. Leave to marinate for 15 minutes.

Meanwhile, heat the oil in a wok or frying pan and gently cook the chilli flakes and garlic for 1 minute, then add the lemon, black pepper and chickpeas. When the chickpeas are hot, switch off the heat.

Preheat the grill to medium-high and line a grill pan with foil. Transfer the cod to the grill pan and cook for 4–5 minutes or until the fish flakes easily.

Turn the heat back on under the chickpeas, mash to break up a little, then add the spinach, fold through and cook for 1–2 minutes, just enough to wilt the leaves.

Stir in the yogurt, divide between 2 warmed plates and top with the spiced cod.

SERVES 6 *Ready in:* 1 hour

2 large sweet potatoes, sliced lengthways into 6
2 large Cypriot (or waxy) potatoes, sliced
  lengthways into 6
6 tbsp olive oil
3 pieces of monkfish tail, 225g each
75g wholemeal breadcrumbs
4 tsp freshly chopped coriander
4 tsp freshly chopped parsley
4 tsp freshly snipped chives
Sea salt and freshly ground black pepper
2 limes, cut into wedges, to serve

FOR THE SALSA
1 orange, segmented, juice reserved
1 apple, cored
2 fresh red chillies, deseeded
1 clove garlic
8 fresh mint leaves
1 tbsp lemon juice

Preheat the oven to 220°C/fan 200°C/gas 8.

Place the sweet potatoes and potatoes in a shallow baking tray. Drizzle over 2 tbsp olive oil and season well with salt and pepper. Toss together well. Roast for 20 minutes. Reduce the temperature to 190°C/fan 170°C/gas 5.

Meanwhile for the salsa either blitz all the ingredients to a chunky sauce or coarsely chop, whichever you prefer.

Brush the monkfish with 2 tbsp olive oil. Toss together the breadcrumbs with the fresh herbs and add any remaining oil. Mix well.

Top each fillet with the breadcrumbs, arrange evenly on a baking tray and drizzle with the remaining oil.

Roast in the oven alongside the potatoes for a further 20 minutes.

Serve with a spoonful of the salsa and garnish with the fresh herbs.

Served here with spinach rice (*see* p.98) and fresh steamed green beans. Capers, lemon juice, olive oil and fish, just a perfect combination. On a busy work day night this simple recipe will restore you, without needing any effort at all.

SERVES 4 *Ready in:* 25 minutes

4 x 150g fresh swordfish steaks, 3cm thick
5 tbsp olive oil
3 tbsp lemon juice
1 tsp caster sugar
1 clove garlic, finely chopped

1 tbsp drained capers, chopped if large
1 tbsp freshly chopped oregano
1 tbsp freshly chopped flat leaf parsley
Sea salt and freshly ground black pepper

Place the fish steaks in a shallow dish and brush both sides with 1 tbsp olive oil and some seasoning.

Mix together the lemon juice, sugar, remaining olive oil, capers and herbs in a bowl. Season with salt and pepper.

Preheat a hot griddle pan or grill, or prepare a barbecue. Cook the swordfish steaks for 2–3 minutes then turn them over and cook for a further 3–4 minutes or until just cooked.

Serve each steak with a spoonful of the herb dressing drizzled over.

TUNA, COUSCOUS AND GREEN BEAN SALAD

SERVES 1 *Ready in:* 15 minutes

100g cooked couscous (or pourgouri, *see* p.99)
100g steamed green beans, refreshed and drained
50g cherry tomatoes, halved
1 tbsp freshly chopped flat leaf parsley
75g fresh tuna steak

1 tbsp extra-virgin olive oil
1 tsp lemon juice
Sea salt and freshly ground black pepper, to
    season

Mix together the couscous, beans and tomatoes. Cover and chill until required.

Heat a non-stick pan, then sear the tuna steak for 30 seconds on each side so coloured on the outside but still very pink on the inside. Remove the pan from the heat.

Make the dressing by whisking together the oil, lemon juice and some seasoning to taste.

Pile the couscous salad on a cold plate, top with the warm tuna and drizzle on the dressing. Enjoy.

EASY SEAFOOD STEW

SERVES 4 *Ready in:* 20 minutes

1 quantity of perfect tomato sauce (*see* p.89)
300 ml fish or vegetable stock
½ tsp saffron strands
1 tsp turmeric
12 large prawns

500g clams
1 large squid, cleaned and cut into rings
2 tbsp freshly chopped parsley
Sea salt and freshly ground black pepper, to
    season

In a large pan warm the tomato sauce, then pour in the stock, add the saffron and turmeric. Cook gently for 10 minutes.

Add the prawns and clams, cover and cook for 3–4 minutes then add the squid.

Cover and cook for a further 3–4 minutes or until the clams are all open (discarding any that do not) and all is piping hot.

Scatter with parsley and serve immediately.

Turmeric is an amazing spice. It has a bright yellow colour and comes from the root of the curcuma plant. It has wonderful anti-inflammatory properties: it aids in the relief of arthritis; is anti-carcinogenic; it protects your heart and can lower cholesterol (and including some freshly ground black pepper increases absorption by 100 per cent!). Turmeric aids indigestion, weight loss and depression. It is the rock star of the spice world and you should get into the habit of adding a teaspoon of turmeric into all your foods. You will really feel the benefit.

Tuna is such a meaty fish that I have tricked my youngest son Zeno into eating it. Try and get the freshest tuna you can and just cook it lightly. The caper sauce works wonderfully with all types of fish and seafood. I like it with large prawns or chunks of halibut or cod too.

MAKES 8 *Ready in:* 30 minutes

4 fresh tuna steaks, 175g, cut into bold chunks
2 red onions, peeled
2 red or green peppers, halved, deseeded
Olive oil, for basting
2 juicy lemons, halved
1 cucumber
3 ripe tomatoes
2 spring onions

Fresh bunches of coriander and parsley
1 tbsp olives

FOR THE CAPER SAUCE:
Juice of 1 large lemon
6 tbsp olive oil
75g capers in brine, rinsed, finely chopped
4-8 fresh pitta bread

First make the salad: dice and mix together cucumber, ripe tomatoes and spring onions for scooping into warmed pitta pockets. Add torn coriander or parsley, olives too.

Toss the tuna chunks in a bowl with enough olive oil to lightly coat. Cut the onions into quarters, separating the wedges. Cut the pepper halves into chunks. Now starting with onion, thread the larger wedges onto skewers alternating with the tuna and pepper. Just before cooking season with salt and pepper.

Make the caper sauce by shaking all ingredients together in a lidded jar.

When ready to eat place the kebabs over the glowing hot coals on the barbeque for approximately 2–3 minutes or until cooked to your preference, basting with olive oil and squeezing over the lemon juice. You do not want the fish to dry out or overcook.

Warm the pitta breads, split open to form a pocket, fill with salad and then the tuna and vegetables. Drizzle the caper sauce into the pitta pocket and enjoy.

GREEK SPICED PRAWNS

SERVES 4 *Ready in:* 10 minutes

500g spinach, washed
2 tbsp olive oil
3 cloves of garlic, chopped
300g cherry tomatoes
1 tsp ground turmeric
1 tsp ground coriander

½ tsp chilli flakes
500g raw king prawns
Zest and juice of 1 lemon
A bunch of coriander leaves, chopped
Sea salt and freshly ground black pepper, to
season

Heat a large frying pan or wok, add the spinach and toss until it just starts to wilt. Transfer to a bowl and set aside.

Add the oil to the pan and gently fry the garlic for 1 minute then add the tomatoes and spices. Cook for a few minutes, stirring every now and then.

Increase the heat and add the prawns and lemon zest. Cook, tossing the prawns around, for a couple of minutes or until they become pink.

Add the lemon juice and return the spinach to the pan with the coriander. Stir and serve.

TONIA'S PRAWNS

Prawns are such a wonderful low fat protein, I always have a pack or two of frozen raw prawns in the freezer just in case I need to whip up a quick supper. It is best to use the raw (grey) prawns not the cooked (pink) prawns, as they can get tough.

SERVES 2 *Ready in:* 20 minutes

1 batch of my perfect tomato sauce (*see* p.89)
225-250g raw prawns (any type, small or king
sized) washed and drained.
150g feta cheese (more or less to taste)

Freshly ground black pepper
Small bunch of parsley, chopped to serve
(optional)

Once you have made your tomato sauce (or if using a batch you have frozen), make sure it is hot then add the prawns and simmer on a low heat till they have turned pink and are cooked though.

I serve straight from the pan but if you want you can put in a serving bowl, crumble over the feta cheese, sprinkle on the pepper and parsley and it is ready to eat.

Serve with some brown rice or chunks of wholemeal bread or if you prefer a lighter meal a green salad or some steamed green beans.

SERVES 4 *Ready in:* 50 minutes

500g mixed seafood (scallops, prawns, squid, mussels; could also include white fish if you like)
250g wholemeal lumaconi rigati (giant pasta shells) or penne
4 cloves garlic, chopped finely
5 shallots, diced
1 large courgette, diced
1 red pepper, 1 yellow pepper diced

Large glass white wine
2 tsp chopped fresh thyme
½ tsp turmeric
Juice and zest of 1 lemon
Small bunch of chopped fresh parsley
150g crumbled feta cheeese (optional)

Preheat oven to 180°C/fan 160°C/gas 4.

Bring a large pan of water to the boil and cook the lumaconi for 5 minutes. Drain and set aside.

Heat the oil in a frying pan and fry the shallots and garlic until soft but not coloured. Add the courgettes and cook until they begin to change colour and soften slightly.

Reduce the heat a little, add the wine and lemon juice and mix through. When the liquid has almost evaporated add the peppers and stir through.

Add the seafood, herbs and spices and black pepper to taste. Cook for a further minute.

Place the pasta in an oven proof dish, scoop side up.

Pour over the seafood mixture. Pour the tomato sauce over the top, spreading evenly to cover the entire dish. Sprinkle the feta over the top.

Bake low in the oven for 30–35minutes – until golden brown.

Serve with a green salad and lemon wedges.

TURKEY AND APPLE PATTIES

These burgers are such a winner with the children. Occasionally, when I want to add some extra nutrition, I blitz a head of broccoli and add that to the mix, or some grated sweet potato. I used turkey mince here as it is very healthy and low fat, but you can also use pork which works well with the apple or lamb mince which makes them extra juicy.

SERVES 4 *Ready in:* 25 minutes

500g minced turkey
2 large cloves of garlic, crushed
1 large onion, finely chopped
2 firm dessert apples, grated
2 tbsp freshly chopped parsley
1 tbsp ground cinnamon

1 tbsp olive oil
4 whole pitta breads
8 tbsp tomato salsa (*see* p.89)
Salad leaves, to serve
Sea salt and freshly ground black pepper, to
  season

Mix together the turkey, garlic, onion, apples, parsley and cinnamon, seasoning with salt and pepper. Divide and form into 4 burgers or patties.

Heat a non-stick frying pan then add the oil and fry over a medium heat for 5–6 minutes on each side – or grill them under a moderate heat, brushing with the oil.

Stuff the burger into the pitta bread with a large helping of salsa and some fresh salad leaves. Enjoy.

EASY CHICKEN PITTAS

SERVES 4 *Ready in:* 30 minutes

400g pack organic chicken breast cut into
  chunks
1 tbsp olive oil
1 tbsp turmeric
1 tbsp paprika
1 tsp chilli flakes (optional)
1 lemon, juice and zest
2 peppers, deseeded and sliced
2 red onions, thickly sliced

20g pack fresh coriander
Sea salt and black pepper

TO SERVE:
8 small wholemeal pittas or 4 large
200ml Greek yogurt
1 pack of wild rocket
Best tomato salsa (*see* p.89)

Place the chicken chunks in a bowl with 1 tsp of oil (reserving the rest) and all the spices and lemon. Toss well, then cover with cling film and chill in the fridge until ready to cook.

Heat the remaining oil in a large frying pan and stir-fry the pepper and onions for 5 minutes, until softened. Tip into a bowl and return the pan to the heat.

Stir fry the chicken gently for 7–8 minutes, until cooked through with no pink meat then return the vegetables to the pan. Cook until sizzling. Stir in the coriander and serve with warmed pittas, Greek yogurt, rocket and salsa.

SERVES 4 *Ready in:* 1½ hours

1.5kg free-range oven ready chicken
2 lemons
1 bay leaf
3 tbsp olive oil
3 tbsp thyme leaves
40 cloves of garlic (approx. 4 bulbs) unpeeled

10 shallots, peeled
150ml retsina or white wine
250ml hot chicken stock
100ml natural Greek yogurt
Salt and freshly ground black pepper

Preheat the oven to 200°C/fan 180°C/gas 6. Place a lemon and the bay leaf in the chicken cavity. Generously season the chicken inside and out with sea salt and pepper, brush 1–2 tbsp oil all over the chicken skin and finally sprinkle on 1 tbsp thyme leaves.

Place the chicken in a large ovenproof casserole and tuck the whole garlic cloves and shallots around the bird. Cut the remaining lemon into quarters and tuck in.

Pour over the retsina and chicken stock, cover the casserole with a tight fitting lid and place over a moderate heat. Bring to a steady simmer then transfer to the oven for 1¼–1½ hours or until the chicken is cooked through and the garlic completely softened.

Carefully transfer the chicken, garlic and shallots to a warmed plate and cover with foil and a couple of dry tea towels. Skim and discard any fat that has risen to the surface of the liquid in the casserole.

Return the casserole to the hob, stir in the remaining thyme and the yogurt. Bring to a gentle simmer for 4–5 minutes. Season to taste and pour into a warm jug. Carve the chicken and serve with the thyme yogurt sauce.

SERVES 2 *Ready in:* 40 minutes

200g tender spinach leaves
450g asparagus spears
2 skinless, boneless free-range chicken breasts
4 tsp green pesto

125g halloumi, cut into slices (or mozzarella, torn into pieces)
250g punnet cherry tomatoes
Sea salt and freshly ground black pepper

Preheat the oven to 200°C/fan 180°C/gas 6.

Fill an ovenproof dish with as much spinach as you can, then layer on the asparagus. Place the chicken breasts on top, spread each with some pesto, dotting the remaining around the vegetables.

Season with some black pepper and a little salt then cover the chicken with some of the cheese, scattering the remainder with the cherry tomatoes around the dish.

Cook for 20 minutes, then check and if becoming too brown cover with foil and cook for a further 5 minutes or until the chicken is tender.

SERVES 4 *Ready in:* 1 hour and 10 minutes

1 1.4kg (3 lb.) oven ready chicken
1 large buffalo tomato, sliced into 8 pieces
1 large onion, sliced
2 tbsp of extra-virgin olive oil

1½ heaped teaspoons of oregano
1½ heaped teaspoons cinnamon
Sea salt and fresh ground pepper

Heat oven to 180˚C/fan 160˚C/gas 4.

Place chicken in roasting dish and rub with 1 tablespoon of olive oil.

Place tomato slices on breast and legs. Sprat the onion rings and place all around chicken.

Season with salt, pepper, oregano and cinnamon.

Drizzle remaining olive oil over chicken and place in oven for 1½ hours or till juices run clear.

right: Cypriot roast chicken (*above*)
and cumin potatoes (*below*)

Since this recipe is slow cooked the whole house fills with the smells of cinnamon and wine. It's a wonderful aroma and really gets the taste buds going. It is very important to use cassia bark NOT cinnamon sticks; this bark looks like it has just come off the tree, not the processed twirled one, as it has a much denser aromatic flavour.

SERVES 4-6 *Ready in:* 1½ hours

1½ whole chicken, jointed into 12 pieces
4–5 tbsp olive oil
10 large Cypriot potatoes, peeled and quartered
  lengthways (if small leave whole)

1 bottle of good quality Cypriot red wine
A handful of cassia bark
Groundnut or sunflower oil for deep fat frying
Sea salt and freshly ground black pepper

Heat some olive oil in a large frying pan or roasting dish and fry the chicken pieces, a few at a time until lightly coloured on all sides.

Meanwhile heat the groundnut oil in a deep frying pan then fry the potatoes, a batch at a time until golden brown. Drain on absorbent kitchen paper. They do not need to be cooked right through at this stage – just coloured.

Once all the chicken pieces are browned, pour on the wine, tuck pieces of cassia bark in amongst the chicken and arrange the potatoes in and around the chicken. Cover tightly and then simmer for 45 minutes–1 hour or until the chicken is very tender, the potatoes soft and tinged red. Season with a little salt and black pepper, to taste.

SERVES 4 *Ready in:* 1 hour

2 tbsp olive oil
8 boneless, skinless chicken thighs, 800g
1 large onion, finely sliced
1 tsp ground cinnamon
1 tsp ground cumin
1 tsp ground ginger
A large pinch saffron strands

500ml chicken stock
3 small preserved lemons, cut into chunks
50g Greek green olives, pitted and roughly
  chopped
200g couscous
Fresh coriander, to garnish
Sea salt and freshly ground black pepper

Heat the oil in a large non-stick pan and brown the chicken pieces. Do this in batches if necessary. Drain and set aside.

Turn the heat to medium and cook the onions until soft and just coloured then sprinkle in all the spices and cook for a further minute.

Return the chicken to the pan and add the stock. Cover and bring to a steady simmer. Cook for 30 minutes then stir in the chopped lemons and olives. Simmer, uncovered for a further 10–15 minutes, allowing the sauce to reduce.

Meanwhile place the couscous in a bowl and pour boiling water over to just cover. Place a clean tea towel over the bowl and leave for 10 minutes. Fluff the couscous up with a fork.

Serve the chicken with the couscous, garnished with freshly chopped coriander.

SERVES 4 *Ready in:* 30 minutes

FOR THE DRESSING:
2 garlic cloves, chopped
A pinch of salt
6 tbsp freshly chopped parsley
175ml extra-virgin olive oil
2 tbsp cider vinegar
2 tbsp lemon juice
½ tsp ugar

3 tbsp olive oil
8 chicken thighs, bone in – or 4 chicken breasts
   if you are on the Ideal Weight diet
3 banana shallots, thinly sliced
400g can chickpeas, drained and rinsed
400g chestnut mushrooms, halved
2 star anise
3 cloves of garlic, sliced
2 tbsp thyme leaves
Sea salt and freshly ground black pepper

Make the parsley dressing simply by shaking all the ingredients together in a clean screw top jam jar. Set aside.

Heat 2 tbsp of the olive oil in a large saucepan or casserole dish over a medium heat. Season the chicken with salt and pepper, add to the hot pan, skin side down and cook for about 6 minutes or until the skin is golden brown.

Turn the chicken over and add the shallots, chickpeas, mushrooms and star anise and cook for 5 minutes.

Turn the chicken back to skin side down, add the garlic and thyme and cook for 15 minutes or so in total; the chicken juices should run clear when pierced with a sharp, tipped knife.

Remove the star anise and serve with some parsley dressing drizzled on top. This is lovely served with spinach rice and a fresh green salad.

OREGANO AND CINNAMON ROAST CHICKEN

SERVES 6 *Ready in:* 40 minutes

1.4kg oven ready free-range chicken
1-2 large beef tomato, thickly sliced into 8
1 large onion, sliced
2 tbsp extra-virgin olive oil

2 tsp dried oregano
2 tsp ground cinnamon
Sea salt and freshly ground black pepper

Preheat the oven to 180°C/fan 160°C/gas 4.

Place chicken in a roasting dish; rub half the olive oil all over its skin. Arrange tomato slices over the breasts and legs. Separate the onion slices and toss around the chicken.

Now scatter on the oregano, cinnamon, and a little salt and pepper to season. Drizzle on the remaining oil over the tomato slices.

Roast for 1½ hour or until the juices run clear. The dish is not elegant but rustic, delicious.

BRAISED CHICKEN WITH VEGETABLES

SERVES 4–6 *Ready in:* 1½ hours

2kg corn-fed free-range chicken, jointed into 4
200ml extra-virgin olive oil
100g loukaniko sausages, sliced (or use smoked bacon lardons)
12 baby new potatoes
2 artichoke hearts, cut into 8 pieces
12 baby onions or shallots

6 garlic cloves
500ml chicken stock
1 fennel bulb, trimmed and cut into 8
12 chestnut mushrooms
2 sprigs of fresh thyme
1 bay leaf
Sea salt and freshly ground black pepper

Season the chicken joints with salt and pepper. Heat half the oil in a large casserole dish and brown the chicken joints all over. Remove and set aside.

Add the loukaniko, potatoes, artichoke hearts and garlic to the hot oil and let them lightly colour for 3 minutes.

Return the chicken to the dish with half the stock. Cover and cook for 10 minutes.

Add the remaining vegetables and herbs, check the seasoning and pour in the remaining stock. Cover and cook for 20 minutes.

Discard the thyme and bay leaf, remove the chicken with a slotted spoon and place on a warm serving dish. Arrange the vegetables around the chicken.

Whisk a little more oil into the sauce and pour over the chicken. Serve.

SERVES 4 *Ready in:* 1 hour

4 cm piece of ginger root, grated
2 cloves of garlic, crushed
1 onion, finely chopped
300 ml Greek 2% yogurt
4 chicken breasts, skinned
2 cinnamon sticks
1 bay leaf
6 cloves

8 black peppercorns
3 cardamoms, peeled and crushed
Juice and zest of 2 lemons
½ tsp chilli powder
1 tsp cumin seeds
Sea salt
1 lemon sliced

Mix together the ginger, garlic, 1 onion and add to the yoghurt. Spread this mixture all over the chicken pieces and leave to marinate for 5 hours (or overnight).

Mix together the cinnamon, bay leaf, cloves, peppercorns and cardamoms. Mix with the lemon juice, chilli powder and cumin seeds. Make slashes with a sharp knife on the chicken pieces and smear them with the mixture. Sprinkle with salt and leave to stand for 1 hour.

From this point there are two ways to cook the chicken:

1. Grill the chicken breasts for about 20–30 minutes, basting frequently and turning chicken once about ½ way through the cooking time.

2. Transfer the chicken and marinade to an ovenproof dish and cook in a preheated oven, at 180°C/fan 160°C/gas 4, for about 40 minutes, or until cooked through.

Garnish with the lemon slices and any remaining onion rings and serve with spinach rice or cracked bulgar wheat.

CHICKEN, BUTTER BEAN AND WALNUT SALAD

SERVES 2 *Ready in:* 30 minutes

200g skinless chicken breast, cut into 2cm pieces
1 sprig rosemary, leaves picked and finely
   chopped
1 sprig lemon thyme, leaves picked and finely
   chopped
3 cloves garlic, finely chopped
1 tbsp olive oil
150g green beans, trimmed
½ x 400g tin butter beans, rinsed and drained
½ red onion, thinly sliced
60g walnuts

FOR THE DRESSING
3 tbsp olive oil
Juice of ½ lemon
2 tbsp wholegrain mustard
1 tbsp runny honey
½ clove garlic, crushed

Place the chicken, rosemary, lemon, thyme, garlic and olive oil in a large bowl and toss together until coated in the oil.

Place a large non-stick frying pan over a medium-high heat and tip in the chicken pieces (in batches if wished). Cook, stirring, for about 10 minutes or until the chicken is browned on all sides and cooked through.

Meanwhile, bring a large pan of water to the boil and add the green beans. Boil for 2 minutes and then add the butter beans and cook for a further 2 minutes until the green beans are just tender and the butter beans are well heated through. Drain well.

Make the dressing by whisking together the olive oil, lemon juice, mustard, honey and crushed garlic in a small bowl.

Mix together the warm chicken, beans, sliced red onion and walnuts in a shallow serving bowl. Pour over the dressing and toss gently.

SERVES 4 *Ready in:* 10 minutes

4 x 100g lamb steaks
Sea salt and black pepper
2 tsp ground cumin
1 tsp ground turmeric
2 tbsp olive oil
2 tbsp sesame seeds
2 tsp Greek honey

75g rocket leaves
1kg watermelon, peeled and cut into chunks
1 small red onion, halved and thinly sliced
1 small pack parsley
Juice of 1 lemon
A drizzle of pomegranate molasses (optional)

If you have time before, rub the lamb steaks with a little olive oil and the spices a few hours before or overnight.

Heat 1 tbsp olive oil in a non-stick pan and cook the lamb for 3 minutes on each side.

Turn off the heat, add the sesame seeds and honey to the hot pan, coat the lamb well.

Mix the rocket, watermelon, onion and parsley together, then divide onto 4 plates.

Slice each steak and place on top of the salad. Drizzle with pan juices and lemon juice. Serve immediately.

SERVES 4 *Ready in:* 25 minutes

FOR THE PATTIES:
500g minced lamb
50g grated sweet potato
50g fresh breadcrumbs
2 tbsp natural Greek yogurt
1 tsp ground cumin
2 tsp ground coriander
2 plump garlic cloves, crushed
2 tbsp freshly chopped mint leaves
Olive oil, for brushing

FOR THE DIP:
200g natural Greek yogurt
3 tbsp wholemeal tahini dip
Juice of 2 lemons
1 clove of garlic, crushed
¼ tsp hot chilli powder, or to taste
¼ tsp ground coriander
1 tsp sea salt

For the patties, mix together all the ingredients to blend well. Divide into 16 balls and roll each ball on a board with cupped hands to form into oval patties. Thread onto 4 metal skewers (or leave as mini patties).

Brush the patties with oil then cook on a griddle for 3–4 minutes on each side. Do not be tempted to turn until they are well sealed else the patties will stick to the grill or pan.

If you prefer you can place all the patties on a greased, lined oven tray and bake in the oven for 40 minutes at 180°C/fan 160°C/gas 4.

Beat all the ingredients for the dip together and serve with the patties.

These are called 'babousakia' in Greek which means 'little shoes'.

SERVES 2 AS A MAIN COURSE OR 4 AS A MEZE *Ready in:* 1 hour

2 aubergines
4 tbsp olive oil
1 onion, finely chopped
250g lean minced lamb
3 tbsp tomato puree
3 cloves garlic, chopped
½ tsp ground cinnamon

1 tsp dried oregano or 1 tbsp freshly chopped
5 large ripe tomatoes, chopped
100ml dry red wine or lamb stock
125g feta cheese, crumbled
Sea salt and freshly ground black pepper, to
  season

Preheat the oven to 200°C/fan 180°C/gas 6.

Cut the aubergines in half lengthways and using a spoon, scoop out the flesh of each, leaving a 1cm border. Rub the shells with the olive oil then sit them upright, snugly, in a shallow ovenproof dish. Cover with foil and bake for 15–20 minutes.

Meanwhile coarsely chop the aubergine flesh. Heat 2 tbsp oil in a large pan, add the aubergine and onion and fry for 3–4 minutes until softened. Add the lamb, breaking it up and cook gently until the meat is browned and crumbly.

Stir in the tomato puree, garlic, cinnamon, oregano, tomatoes and wine. Mix well and simmer for 15 minutes or until the delicious juices have reduced to just a couple of tablespoons.

Divide the lamb mixture into the aubergine shells and return to the oven, covered for 20 minutes.

Remove the foil, sprinkle on the feta and cook for 5–10 minutes more to tinge the feta golden. Serve warm as a main or cold as part of a meze.

SERVES 6-8 (6 GREEKS, 8 NON-GREEKS!) *Ready in:* 4 ½ hours, plus resting time

2.5 kg leg or shoulder of lamb
olive oil
Sea salt and freshly ground black pepper
1 bulb of garlic separated into cloves
4–6 bay leaves

4 lemons, cut into quarters lengthways
1 tsp of ground cinnamon
150g Greek Kalkidis olives
Optional 1kg of Cypriot potatoes washed peeled
and cut lengthways into quarters

Put your oven on as high as it will go.

Score the fat of the lamb in a criss-cross manner.

In a deep-sided baking dish put half the garlic cloves, 2 of the bay leaves and the lemon quarters into the bottom of the dish.

Place the lamb on top, drizzle with a good helping of oil, rubbing it in all over, then take the remaining garlic cloves and bay leaves and stuff into the slashed fat of the lamb.

Season well and sprinkle over the cinnamon.

Cover tightly with silver foil.

Place into the oven then turn the temperature down to 170°C/fan 150°C/gas 3½.

Leave to cook for 4 hours.

If you are adding the potatoes, put them around the lamb after 3 hours.

After 4 hours take the foil off the lamb and place to one side.

Roast for a further ½ hour.

Five minutes before you remove the lamb throw in the green olives making sure they are covered in the meat liquor.

Take out of the oven, cover tightly again with foil and a tea towel and allow to rest. I like to carve the lamb in the baking dish and serve it very rustically.

SERVES 4 *Ready in:* 1 hour

1 tbsp olive oil
350g lean shoulder of lamb, diced
2 rashers smokey bacon, roughly chopped
2 onions, chopped
1 celery stalk, chopped
1 large carrot, diced
4 cloves of garlic, finely chopped

1 tsp fennel seeds
2 waxy potatoes, diced
400g can Borlotti beans, drained and rinsed
2 tbsp tomato puree
500ml lamb or vegetable stock
250g fresh baby spinach leaves
Sea salt and freshly ground black pepper

Heat the oil in a large non-stick pan and cook the lamb, bacon, onions, celery and carrot for 5 minutes or until lightly coloured. Add the garlic and fennel seeds and cook for a further minute.

Stir in the potatoes, tomato puree and lamb stock. Cover and simmer gently for at least 45 minutes or until the lamb is tender.

Stir in the spinach, cook for 1–2 minutes to wilt the leaves then ladle into warmed bowls and enjoy.

SERVES 6 *Ready in:* 2 hours

1 butterflied leg of lamb (an average leg of
   lamb weighs 3.5kg, giving you a boneless
   weight of 2kg)

SPICE RUB:

125g almonds, roasted and chopped
3 cloves of garlic, diced
½ tsp turmeric
5 tbsp freshly chopped coriander

5 tbsp freshly chopped mint
½ tsp dried chilli flakes
100ml olive oil
Zest and juice of 2 lemons

Make the rub: blitz the first 6 ingredients in a hand blender or food processor. Add the oil and lemon
zest and juice. Massage this over both sides of the lamb.

Place the lamb, cut side up, on a rack set over a roasting tray and bake in a preheated oven at 190°C/
fan 170°C/gas 5 for 15 minutes. Turn the lamb and roast for another 20 minutes then remove from
the oven and leave to rest for 20 minutes.

FOR THE PARSNIP ROSTI:

400g parsnip, scrubbed and coarsely grated
200g potato, scrubbed and coarsely grated
2 egg whites
1 tsp ground turmeric

½ tsp ground coriander
2 tbsp olive oil
Sea salt and freshly ground black pepper

Place the parsnip and potato in a clean tea towel and twist the towel to squeeze out excess liquid.

Place the parsnip and potato in a bowl with the egg white, spices and olive oil. Mix together well.

Form the mixture into pancake shapes and place on an oiled baking tray and cook alongside the lamb
for 35–45 minutes or until browned and crisp.

This hearty pork bake is so very simple to make: literally throw everything into the dish and put it in the oven, bring it out once it is cooked and serve it rustically straight to the table, with a big Greek salad and lots of yogurt.

SERVES 4 *Ready in:* 2 hours

1kg shoulder of pork, cut into fist size pieces
1kg Cyprus potatoes, quartered
Olive oil to drizzle
2–3 tsp ground cumin

1 tsp ground cinnamon
6 large tomatoes, thickly sliced
3 large onions, sliced
Sea salt and freshly ground black pepper

Preheat the oven to 200°C/fan 180°C/gas 6.

Put the pork and potatoes in a large earthenware dish. Pour a good drizzle of oil into the dish and with clean hands, coat the meat and potatoes well with oil. Add the spices, mix again.

Arrange the tomato and onion slices over the top, pour on a little more oil and season with the salt and pepper.

Cover tightly with foil and cook for around 1 hour then lower the heat to 180°C/fan 160°C/gas 4, remove the foil and cook for 40–45 minutes until nicely browned and the meat is tender.

SERVES 8 AS PART OF A MEZE AND 4 AS A MAIN COURSE *Ready in:* 45 minutes

8 large peppers, assorted colours
120ml olive oil
2 large onions, chopped
100g long grain rice
125g minced pork
2 tbsp freshly chopped parsley
2 tbsp freshly chopped mint

2 tsp ground cinnamon
400g can plum tomatoes (or 4 large fresh
    tomatoes, grated)
Juice of 1 lemon
Sea salt and freshly ground black pepper

Preheat the oven to 180°C/fan 160°C/gas 4.

Neatly slice the tops off the peppers, reserving them for later (or halve the peppers lengthways). Scoop out and discard the seeds.

Heat 3 tbsp olive oil in a large pan and fry the onions until softened. Stir in the rice and pork and continue cooking until the rice becomes transparent, the meat crumbly.

Stir in the herbs, cinnamon and tomatoes. Season with salt and pepper. Cook for 5 minutes.

Spoon the mince and rice mixture into the peppers to about ¾ full. Stand the peppers snugly in a casserole dish (use potato slices to wedge them if necessary to keep upright). Pop their lids back on. Mix together the lemon juice with the remaining olive oil and 6 tbsp water. Pour around the peppers.

Cover loosely with foil and bake in the oven for 30 minutes or until tender.

BEEF STIFADO

....

SERVES 4 *Ready in:* 40 minutes

6 tbsp olive oil
1½ kg lean braising beef, cubed
4 cloves garlic, chopped
5 tbsp red wine vinegar
1½ kg shallots, peeled
3 pieces cinnamon bark

2 bay leaves
1 tsp whole cloves
1½ tsp aniseed (or fennel seeds or 2 star anise)
3 x 400g cans chopped tomatoes
Sea salt and pepper

Heat the olive oil in a large heavy-based pan then brown the cubed meat in batches. Remove and set aside.

Add the shallots to the pan and cook gently until caramelised. Now add the garlic and cook for a further minute or two. Burnt garlic becomes bitter so always take care to add after onions.

Add the vinegar, the spices and tomatoes and season well. Stir in 200ml hot water. Cover tightly and simmer for a minimum of 1½ hours but preferably 2 hours or until the meat is very tender, in a rich, thick sauce.

MEATBALLS A LA GRECQUE

....

SERVES 4 *Ready in:* 40 minutes

1 quantity of perfect tomato sauce (*see* p.89)
500g extra lean minced beef
½ tsp ground cinnamon

1 onion, finely chopped
1 tbsp olive oil
Sea salt and freshly ground black pepper

Use a food processor to finely chop and bind the minced beef, cinnamon and onion together then form the mixture into 16 equal rounds, the size of a walnut.

Heat the oil in a large pan over a medium heat, add the meatballs and cook for 7–8 minutes or nicely browned all over. Remove the meatballs to a plate.

Add the tomato sauce to the pan and bring to a gentle simmer. Return the meatballs, part-cover and simmer for 15 minutes or until the meatballs are cooked through.

Adjust the seasoning to taste and serve.

PUDDINGS, BAKES & CAKES

PEACH WITH BASIL AND ORANGE BLOSSOM YOGURT

Filo pastry is a wonderful vehicle for many flavours, sweet or savoury. I like the unusual mix of peach and basil but you can also put in fruits and spices that you especially like. Strawberries and mint work well or chopped bananas and cinnamon.

SERVES 6 *Ready in:* 40 minutes

6 sheets filo pastry, thawed if frozen
3 tbsp olive oil
3 firm but ripe peaches, skinned, halved and
   stoned
6 large basil leaves
6 tsp Comandaria (optional)

TO SERVE:
100ml natural Greek yogurt
1 tbsp orange blossom water
A sprinkling of ground cinnamon

Preheat the oven to 180°C/fan 160°C/gas 4.

Cut the filo pastry into six 12cm x 12cm squares and brush each with a little olive oil.

Place a basil leaf in the centre of each square, followed by half a peach, cut side up. Pour the Comandaria into each stone cavity.

Bring the four corners together at the top and twist to create a parcel. Place on a baking sheet.

Bake for 20–25 minutes or until golden brown.

Serve immediately with a spoonful of yogurt and a sprinkling of cinnamon.

Everyone loves custard, and in the hot Mediterranean heat they eat it chilled and served with sweets on top. Don't worry if you do not have any, it is just as lovely sprinkled with cinnamon and served with some stewed fruit, or with pear and filo tart.

The stodgy rice pudding you were served at school is a million miles away from this aromatic light pudding that is bursting with Mediterranean flavours. As it has so little sugar I sometimes have it for breakfast with some blueberries and raspberries on top.

SERVES 6–8 *Ready in:* 30 minutes, plus chilling

200g corn flour or rice flour
1.2 litres milk (at room temperature)
6 tbsp rose water or 1 vanilla pod, halved and
   seeds taken out
6 eggs, beaten

Zest 1 lemon
200g caster sugar
Spoon sweets, to decorate (candied walnuts,
   watermelon peel, bergamot or lemon)

Blend the corn flour with a little milk to make a smooth paste. Heat the remaining milk in a saucepan, bringing to a steady simmer. Now, using a wooden spoon, blend in the corn flour paste, sugar, rose water or vanilla and lemon zest, stirring constantly.

Once the custard is smooth reduce the heat. Pour a little of the hot custard onto the beaten eggs, whisking constantly until smooth, not scrambled. Whisk back into the hot custard and continue to heat, stirring until the custard thickens enough to coat the back of the wooden spoon.

Pour the custard into a shallow glass flan dish and leave to cool, then chill until set.

Just before serving, decoratively arrange your favourite assorted sliced spoon sweets over the top.

SERVES 6 *Ready in:* 30 minutes

180g brown pudding rice
50g caster sugar
1 litre semi-skimmed milk
2 heaped tbsp cornflour

4 tbsp orange blossom water or rosewater
Orange peel/rose petals to garnish
Ground cinnamon

Place the rice in a large saucepan and pour on just enough cold water to cover the rice by about 2.5cm. Cover and cook the rice gently until most of the water is absorbed. Now stir in the milk, gradually bring to the boil, then reduce the heat to simmer, covered, for about 20 minutes.

Now for the flavourings. Add more or less to suit your taste buds. Stir the sugar, rice, orange blossom or rose water into the rice. Blend the cornflour with enough milk or water to make a thin paste then stir into the rizogalo.

Bring to the steady simmer stirring, until the mixture thickens.

Divide between individual bowls or one large serving dish. Leave to cool then refrigerate for around 2 hours to firm up.

Just before serving sprinkle with cinnamon and decorate with shavings of orange peel or rose petals.

This is such a strange dessert. It has a magical quality and is so moreish you just can't stop coming back for another slice. It is flavoured with mastic which is a resinous gum exuded by the bark of the mastic tree, which grows on the Greek island of Chios in the Aegean sea. It has amazing anti-bacterial qualities and it is said that if you chew the gum regularly it can help shrink stomach ulcers. It is also a great aid to any digestive disorders. It has a wonderful, slightly bitter, piney flavour.

SERVES 6 *Ready in:* 30 minutes

175g coarse cut semolina
½ tsp mastic
100g flaked almonds

3 tbsp olive oil
1 litre water
175g caster sugar

Mix 2 tbsp semolina with the mastic, crushing, ideally in a pestle and mortar. The semolina prevents the mastic getting sticky. Set aside.

Heat the olive oil in a large saucepan then fry the almonds until golden brown. Set aside 2 tbsp for decoration.

Pour the remaining semolina into the pan and mix well. Stir in the water and sugar. Bring to the boil then simmer gently, stirring constantly until the mixture starts to thicken slightly. Now add the crushed mastic and continue to stir over a moderate heat until the consistency of thick custard.

Pour into a shallow serving dish, sprinkle on the remaining browned almonds and leave to cool.

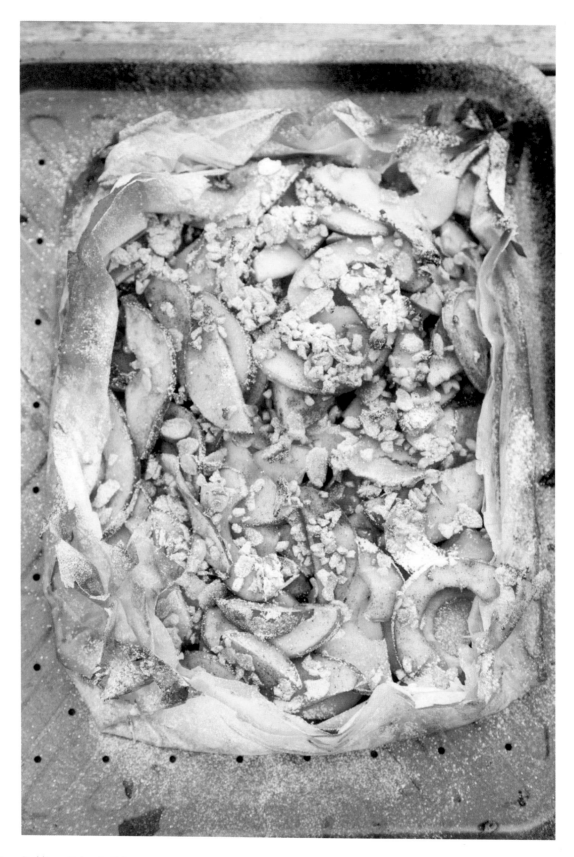

PEAR AND APPLE FILO TART

This always looks so lovely coming straight from the oven to the table, apples, pears, nuts and spices; tastes just as good cold too. You can use whatever filling you like. In the summer, when I have a plum harvest from the tree in the garden I put in plums, or if you have a summer fruit glut of strawberries or blackberries you can use them too.

SERVES 8 *Ready in:* 30 minutes

6 sheets filo pastry
4 tbsp olive oil
100g flaked almonds
50g chopped hazelnuts
50g unrefined brown sugar

3 tsp ground cinnamon
½ tsp ground mastic (optional)
3 dessert apples, peel on, cored and thinly sliced
3 dessert pears, peel on, cored and thinly sliced
Zest and juice of 1 lemon

Preheat the oven to 190°C/fan 170°C/gas 5. Lightly oil a large baking sheet.

Place 2 sheets of filo on the tray, oiling between each sheet, overlapping them slightly. Scatter on a third of the nut mixture, then repeat with another 2 sheets of filo and then another third of the nuts, finishing with the top 2 layers of filo pastry.

In a bowl, mix the remaining nuts with the sliced fruit, sugar and spice then evenly scatter over the top layer of pastry, folding in the pastry edges to form a rustic rim.

Bake for 20 minutes or until the pastry is crisp and golden and the fruit softened. Serve cut into rectangles. Best enjoyed freshly baked and warm.

SERVES 4 *Ready in:* 30 minutes

1 tbsp olive oil
500g fresh figs, washed
300g medul dates (or dried)
1 tsp ground cinnamon, extra for sprinkling

1 tsp ground allspice
Zest and juice of 1 lemon
4 tbsp runny honey

Preheat the oven to 200°C/fan 180°C/gas 6. Oil an ovenproof dish.

Slice the figs in half and prick with a fork on the skin side.

Cut the dates in half and remove the stones. Arrange in the dish alternating with the figs.

Sprinkle over the spices and lemon juice. Drizzle with the honey.

Bake for 20 minutes or until the honey starts to bubble.

Serve warm with Greek yogurt and a sprinkling of cinnamon.

SERVES 4 *Ready in:* 4 hours

1 kg village flour
200ml olive oil
½ packet dried yeast
1 tsp ground cinnamon
1 tsp ground mastic

1 tsp ground mehelpi seeds
100g sesame seeds
2 tsp aniseed seeds
1 tbsp sugar
A pinch of sea salt

Mix all the flour, olive oil, dried yeast, cinnamon, mastic and mehelpi seeds together in a large bowl, adding just enough warm water to bind together to form a smooth dough. Cover and leave in a warm place to prove for 1 hour.

Place the sesame seeds in a sieve and pour on boiling water to rinse. Drain and mix with the aniseed and sugar. Spread into a large shallow dish.

Pinch off a walnut size piece of dough, roll it in to a thin rope or tube about the length of a dinner knife. If it gets sticky; dust with a little more flour. Fold in half then twist two times or make a coiled circle or a snake shape. Roll or dip into the sesame seeds then transfer onto a floured baking sheet.

Bake in a preheated oven 180°C/fan 160°C/gas 4 for 20 minutes. Remove and cool the biscuits. Reduce the oven temperature to 120°C/fan 100°C/gas ½ and return the biscuits to the oven for a further 2 hours. Cool and store in an airtight container.

SERVES 6 *Ready in:* 1 hour

120ml olive oil
100g light brown Muscovado sugar, plus 1tbsp
150g self-raising flour
2 tsp ground cinnamon
3 free-range medium eggs, beaten

2 tbsp milk
2 crisp dessert apples eg Cox, quartered and
    sliced
100g pecan nuts, roughly chopped
75g sultanas

Preheat the oven to 180°C/fan 160°C/gas 4. Oil and line an 18cm round, loose-bottomed or spring-form cake tin.

Place the olive oil, sugar, (reserving 1 tbsp) and eggs into a large bowl and mix together well.

Sift in the flour and cinnamon and fold in to form a smooth batter. Add a splash of milk to slacken, if required.

Now add all but a handful of the apples with the nuts and sultanas to the cake mix. Pour into the prepared tin and scatter the remaining apples and 1 tbsp sugar over the surface.

Bake for 1 hour until well risen and golden brown and a skewer inserted in the centre comes out clean. Cool a little in the tin before inverting onto a wire rack to cool.

HEALTHY FRUIT CAKE

....

SERVES 8–10 SLICES *Ready in:* 1 hour

3 ripe bananas, mashed
2 medium free-range eggs, beaten
50g ground almonds
100g walnut pieces
150g sultanas
2 dessert apples, finely chopped
100g pitted prunes, chopped (optional)

200ml natural Greek yogurt
2 tsps ground cinnamon
1 tsp ground allspice
150g wholemeal flour
1 tbsp baking powder
200ml herbal tea (mint or camomile) to slacken
   the mix

Preheat the oven to 180°C/fan 160°C/gas 4. Oil and line a 1kg loaf tin.

In a bowl or food processor beat together the bananas, eggs and ground almonds. Stir in the walnuts, sultanas, prunes and yogurt.

Now add all the dry ingredients and mix well, adding as much tea as needed to slacken the mixture.

Pour into the prepared loaf tin and bake for 45 minutes or until firm to touch and a skewer inserted in the centre comes out clean. Cool a little in the tin before inverting on a wire rack to cool.

CINNAMON, FIG AND BANANA MUFFINS

....

MAKES 8–10 *Ready in:* 1 hour

4 ripe bananas
2 medium free-range eggs
5 tbsp olive oil
50g muscovado sugar
120ml milk

1 tsp ground cinnamon
150g wholemeal flour
1½ tbsp baking powder
50g dried figs, chopped
25g sunflower seeds

Preheat the oven to 180°C/fan 160°C/gas 4. Line a muffin tray with 8–10 large paper muffin cases.

In a large bowl mash 3 bananas then beat together with the eggs, oil, sugar and milk.

Now add all the dry ingredients with the figs and seeds. Mix to just combine – do not overmix at this stage.

Spoon 2 heaped tbsp into each muffin case and decorate each with a slice of banana. Bake for 20 minutes or until risen, nicely coloured and springy to the touch. Allow to cool. Serve freshly made and preferably warm.

MY GREENGROCER'S CAKE (GLUTEN-FREE)

This cake is for all my coeliac and wheat intolerant friends who come to tea. I have taken inspiration from the wonderful Sabrina Ghayour who has an amazing wheat free cake in her book *Persiana* which I adore; actually I adore all her recipes.

MAKES 8 SLICES *Ready in:* 1 hour and 10 minutes

3 eggs
100g demerara sugar
70ml rose water
200g ground almonds
150g desiccated coconut
100g raw virgin coconut oil
2 heaped tablespoons ground cinnamon
2 courgettes, finely grated
1 large carrot, finely grated
100g chopped or flaked almonds
100g sultanas (or cranberries)

ROSE YOGURT:
500ml Greek yogurt 2% fat or full fat.
50ml rose water
50g icing sugar

TO DECORATE:
Icing sugar for dusting
Dried rose petals to sprinkle on top.

Preheat your oven to 150°C/fan 130°C/gas 2. Line a circular cake tin.

Beat the eggs and sugar together, add all the other ingredients and mix really well.

Pour into the cake tin and bake for an hour.

For the rose yogurt, mix together all the ingredients and serve on the side of the cake.

Puddings, Bakes & Cakes

MAKES 2 ROUND LOAVES *Ready in:* 1 hour

Fresh yeast
1 tsp caster sugar
1kg wholemeal flour
2 tbsp olive oil
1 heaped tsp ground cinnamon

1 tbsp runny honey
2 tsp salt
400g dried figs, finely chopped
100g walnut pieces

Preheat the oven to 200°C/fan 180°C/gas 6. Lightly oil and line a medium size loose-bottomed cake tin.

In a large bowl, combine 200ml warm water with the yeast and sugar. Stir to dissolve, leave to stand for 5 minutes or until the yeast is foamy. Stir in 200g wholemeal flour. Cover the bowl with a clean towel and leave in a warm place for 45 minutes or until the mixture is thick and bubbly.

Add 600g flour, 1 tbsp oil, honey, salt and 100ml warm water and work well to combine all the ingredients. Tip out onto a floured board and knead for 5–8 minutes adding more flour if required, until the dough is smooth and elastic. Fold dough over onto the figs and nuts and knead to combine well. Place in a well-oiled clean bowl, turning the dough to coat with some oil. Cover the bowl and leave in a warm place for about 2 hours or until the dough doubles in size.

Punch the dough down, let it rest for 10 minutes then tip out onto a lightly floured board. Cut the dough in half. Shape each piece into a 15cm round loaf. Place the 2 loaves onto an oiled baking tray. Cover and leave to rise for 45 minutes or until doubled in size.

With a serrated knife, make several slashes in the top of each loaf. Brush the loaves with the remaining oil. Bake for 30–35 minutes or until the bottom sounds hollow when tapped. Cool for 10 minutes on the baking sheet then transfer to wire racks to cool completely.

MAKES 8-10 SLICES *Ready in:* 1 hour and 10 minutes

70 ml olive oil
3 eggs, beaten
4–5 large ripe bananas, mashed
50g Greek yogurt
200g walnut pieces
300g chopped dates (the pitted square packs are
    great)

400g wholemeal spelt or rye flour
1 heaped tbsp baking powder
3tsp ground cinnamon
Cup of green tea cooled, to use to slacken mix

Preheat the oven to 180°C/fan 160°C/gas 4. Lightly oil a 23cm spring-clip ring cake tin or a lined 2 litre loaf tin.

Pour the oil in a bowl, then beat in the eggs and mashed banana and yogurt, and beat until smooth (this can be done in a food processor).

Stir in the walnuts and dates then fold in the flour, baking powder and cinnamon. If the mixture seems a little dry, add some green tea (or milk) to slacken to a thick batter consistency.

Pour into an oiled and lined tin and bake in the middle of the oven for 45 minutes or until well risen and browned. To test when cooked insert the point of a sharp knife or skewer; it should come out clean.

TONIA'S TIP:
Bananas are a rich source of iron and fibre, dried dates are a good source of potassium, copper and magnesium, and walnuts are an excellent source of omega-3 essential fatty acids, so this cake gets the thumbs up for healthy skin.

SERVES 10 SLICES *Ready in:* 1 hour 10 minutes

75 ml olive oil
50g caster sugar
4 free-range medium eggs, separated
120ml natural Greek yogurt
250g wholemeal flour
1 tbsp baking powder

1 tsp ground cinnamon
100g flaked almonds
100g dried organic apricots, chopped
Juice of 1 lemon
1 tsp bicarbonate of soda

Preheat the oven to 170°C/fan 150°C/gas 3. Lightly oil and line a medium size loose-bottomed cake tin.

Beat the olive oil, sugar and egg yolks together in a large bowl. Add the yogurt and mix in well.

Fold in the flour, baking powder, cinnamon, almonds (reserving a handful) and apricots.

In a clean bowl, whisk the egg whites until forming soft snowy mounds. Mix together the lemon juice and bicarbonate of soda and fold into the egg whites then gently fold this into the cake mixture.

Spoon the mixture into the prepared tin. Scatter on the reserved flaked almonds. Bake for 50–55 minutes or until the cake is well risen and golden and a skewer inserted in the centre comes out clean.

Cool slightly in the tin before turning out onto a cooling rack.

SERVES 10-12 SLICES *Ready in:* 1 hour

100ml olive oil
100g demerara sugar
4 free-range medium eggs, beaten
200ml natural Greek yogurt
Zest and juice of 1 lemon
500g wholemeal or spelt flour
1 tbsp baking powder
1 tsp ground allspice

2 tbsp poppy seeds
200g flaked almonds
4–5 tbsp green tea or milk, to slacken

FOR THE SYRUP:
Zest and juice of 2 lemons
100g demerara sugar

Preheat the oven to 180°C/fan 160°C/gas 4. Oil and line a 1kg loaf tin.

Beat the olive oil, sugar and eggs together in a large bowl, then whisk in the yogurt and mix together well.

Fold in the flour, baking powder, allspice, poppy seeds and almonds to form a smooth mixture. Then mix in the zest and juice of the lemon, adding a splash of milk or tea to slacken to a dropping consistency, if required.

Spoon the mixture into the prepared tin. Bake for 40 minutes or until the cake is well risen and golden and a skewer inserted in the centre comes out clean.

Meanwhile mix together the lemon zest and juice with the demerara sugar and spoon over the hot cake as soon as it comes out of the oven. Leave to stand for 30 minutes to allow the syrup to seep through.

We all know some foods are better for us than others. Here's some additional information on a few truly 'wonder'-ful and health-giving foods.

OLIVE OIL

NUTRITIONAL INFORMATION

Vitamin E, Vitamin K, Iron, Monounsaturated fat

HEALTH BENEFITS

- Reduces risk of type 2 diabetes when compared to low fat diet
- Slows the ageing of the heart by keeping arteries healthy
- Lowers bad and regulates good cholesterol
- Known to reduce inflammation
- Can lower risk of stroke
- Can reduce the risk of cancers including skin and breast cancers
- Rich in antioxidants
- Can reduce the risk of rheumatoid arthritis
- Aids in alleviation of Hypertension (high blood pressure)
- Enhances insulin sensitivity and improves blood sugar control
- May reduce risk of Alzheimer's disease
- Shown to reduce levels of obesity, in spite of having a high calorific content
- Aids in calcium absorption
- Improves bone mineralization
- Aids in the protection against osteoporosis onset

TAHINI

NUTRITIONAL INFORMATION

Vitamin B1, Vitamin B2, Vitamin B3, Vitamin B5, Vitamin E, Calcium, Phosphorus, Magnesium, Potassium, Iron, Dietary Fibre, Omega-3, Omega-6

HEALTH BENEFITS

- Prevents anaemia
- Aids liver detoxification
- Maintains healthy skin
- Maintains healthy muscle tone
- Easy to digest, assisting in weight management
- Can increase energy levels

GARLIC

NUTRITIONAL INFORMATION

Carbohydrates, Vitamin B1 (Thiamin), Vitamin B2 (Riboflavin), Vitamin B5 (Pantothenic Acid), Vitamin B6, Vitamin C, Calcium, Dietary Fibre, Magnesium, Phosphorus, Manganese, Selenium, Iron, Potassium, Copper, Zinc

HEALTH BENEFITS

- Increases immune function
- May reduce risk of colon cancer
- Known to provide protection against heart disease
- Aids in alleviation of cardiovascular disease
- Known to reduce and aid in the treatment of high blood pressure
- Can promote eye health
- Aids in the protection against osteoporosis
- Can help prevent stroke
- Reduces risk of type 2 diabetes
- Can reduce frequency of migraine headaches
- Offers alleviation of Premenstrual Syndrome (PMS)
- Antioxidant protection
- Found to be helpful in prevention of epileptic seizures
- Aids in prevention of alopecia (spot baldness)
- Crushed raw garlic contains an antibiotic called allicin, thus, it is good to eat garlic when you have a cold or flu
- As a blood thinner, garlic is thought to promote cardiovascular health and reduce the chance of heart attack
- Garlic is also a cholesterol-lowering food

TOMATOES

NUTRITIONAL INFORMATION
Vitamin A, Lycopene, Vitamin C, Vitamin K, Manganese, Potassium

Less than 5%
Vitamin B6, Vitamin B9 (Folic Acid)

HEALTH BENEFITS
- Increases protection against bacterial and viral infections
- Strengthens the immune system
- Reduces the risk of many cancers including colon, breast, prostate
- Offers protection against heart disease
- Aids in alleviation of cardiovascular disease
- Aids in alleviation of hypertension
- Keeps the skin healthy
- Can offer some protection against Alzheimer's disease
- Aids in the protection against osteoporosis
- Beneficial for stroke prevention
- Effective for weight control diets
- Excellent antioxidant properties
- Found to aid in prevention of epileptic seizures
- Aids in the prevention of alopecia (spot baldness)
- Tomatoes are high in the powerful cancer-fighting antioxidant lycopene, especially prevalent in cooked tomatoes

CHICKPEAS

NUTRITIONAL INFORMATION
Vitamin A, Vitamin C, Vitamin E, Vitamin K, Choline, Vitamin B1, Vitamin B2, Vitamin B3, Vitamin B5, Vitamin B9, Potassium, Phosphorus, Magnesium, Calcium, Iron, Selenium

Less than 5%
Zinc, Manganese

HEALTH BENEFITS
- Reduces cholesterol and risk of heart disease
- Strengthens bones and bone health
- Aids vasodilation and healthy blood pressure
- Aids weight management as a bulking agent
- Prevents some digestive disorders
- Reduces risk of coronary heart disease
- Lowers iron deficiency
- Stabilises and lowers blood sugar
- Protects against osteoporosis
- May modulate oestrogen and lower risk of breast cancer and aid in hormone production

LEMON

NUTRITIONAL INFORMATION
Vitamin C, Potassium, Water

Less than 5%
Calcium, Iron, Magnesium, Vitamin B1 (Thiamin), Vitamin B6, Vitamin B9 (Folic Acid)

HEALTH BENEFITS
- Increases immune function
- Offers protection against heart disease
- Aids in alleviation of cardiovascular disease
- Aids in alleviation of hypertension
- Aids in the protection against osteoporosis
- Beneficial for stroke prevention
- A known anti-inflammatory
- Flavonoids found in lemons are believed to have antioxidant and anti-cancer properties

CHILLI

NUTRITIONAL INFORMATION

Vitamin A, Vitamin B6, Vitamin B9 (Folic Acid), Vitamin C, Vitamin K, Magnesium, Manganese, Iron, Potassium, Copper

HEALTH BENEFITS

- The capsaicin in peppers acts as a vasodilator, helping to increase blood flow to all parts of the body and lower blood pressure
- Offers increased protection from bacterial and viral infections
- Increases immune function
- Reduces some cancer risk
- Offers protection against heart disease
- Can slow the ageing process
- Aids in DNA repair and protection
- Aids in alleviation of cardiovascular disease
- Aids in alleviation of hypertension
- Aids in protection against Alzheimer's disease
- Offers osteoporosis protection
- Beneficial for stroke prevention
- Reduces risk of type 2 diabetes
- A known metabolism booster
- Reduces the frequency of migraine headaches
- Offers alleviation of Premenstrual Syndrome (PMS)
- Delivers antioxidant protection
- Can aid in prevention of epileptic seizures
- Aids in the prevention of alopecia (spot baldness)

AUBERGINES

NUTRITIONAL INFORMATION

Vitamin B1 (Thiamin), Dietary Fibre, Manganese.

HEALTH BENEFITS

- Aubergines are high in antioxidants and are thought to contain chemicals which can help reduce cholesterol
- Aids in the protection against osteoporosis
- Offers antioxidant protection
- Aids in prevention of epileptic seizures
- Aids in prevention of alopecia (spot baldness)

YOGURT

NUTRITIONAL INFORMATION

Nutrition varies by brand!
Vitamin B2, Vitamin B5, Vitamin B6, Vitamin B12, Vitamin D, Calcium, Potassium, Phosphorus, Zinc

HEALTH BENEFITS

- Aids in weight management by creating less cortisol
- Aids healthy digestion
- Contains beneficial bacteria
- Helpful in weight loss, healthy snack making you feel fuller
- Boosts the immune system
- Protects teeth and gums
- Probiotic which can strengthen immune system and functionality
- Prevents and treats osteoporosis
- Increases bone mass
- Can discourage vaginal infections
- Aids recovery after working out
- Prevents hypertension

FETA

NUTRITIONAL INFORMATION

Vitamin A, Vitamin B1, Vitamin B2, Vitamin B3, Vitamin B6, Vitamin B9, Vitamin B12, Calcium, Protein, Iron, Phosphorus, Selenium, Zinc

HEALTH BENEFITS

- Has one third of the calories and fat compared to most cheeses
- Aids in tooth and bone strength
- Helps metabolise fats
- Prevents heart disease by keeping red blood cells healthy
- Increases immune system functionality

ARTICHOKE

NUTRITIONAL INFORMATION

Vitamin B3 (Niacin), Vitamin B9 (Folic Acid), Vitamin C, Vitamin K, Magnesium, Phosphorus, Manganese, Copper

HEALTH BENEFITS

- Increases immune function
- Reduces some cancer risk
- Offers protection against heart disease
- Aids in regulation of blood sugar and insulin dependence
- Can slow the progression of AIDS
- Found to slow the effects of ageing
- Offers DNA repair and protection
- Aids in alleviation of cardiovascular disease
- Aids in alleviation of high blood pressure
- Offers protection against Alzheimer's disease
- Aids in the protection against osteoporosis
- Reduces the risk of type 2 diabetes
- Reduces frequency of migraine headaches
- Offers alleviation of premenstrual syndrome (PMS)
- Offers antioxidant protection
- Aids in prevention of epileptic seizures
- Aids in prevention of alopecia (spot baldness)
- Artichokes are known for the detoxification and regeneration of the liver, reducing sugar and cholesterol levels in the blood, and for aiding the gall bladder in the metabolism of fat.

EGGS

NUTRITIONAL INFORMATION

Vitamin A, Vitamin B2, Vitamin B5, Vitamin B6, Vitamin B12, Vitamin D, Vitamin E, Vitamin K, Phosphorus, Selenium, Calcium, Zinc, Choline, Protein

HEALTH BENEFITS

- Aids healthy baby development during pregnancy
- Can raise levels of good cholesterol
- Maintains healthy skin
- Boosts energy metabolism
- Can aid mental functioning
- Strengthens nervous and immune system
- Aids in healthy reproductive organs
- Slows degeneration of the eye, and contains antioxidants which aid eye health
- Can increase muscle mass
- Can lower blood pressure
- Optimises bone health
- Known to aid in weight loss

ONIONS

NUTRITIONAL INFORMATION

Vitamin B6, Vitamin C, Dietary Fibre, Manganese.

Less than 5%
Potassium, Selenium

HEALTH BENEFITS

- Can increase immune function
- Can lower cholesterol
- Offers protection against heart disease and blood vessels
- Osteoporosis protection and increases bone density
- Gives antioxidant protection against fatty acids in the body
- Has anti-inflammatory properties
- Aids in prevention of epileptic seizures
- Aids in prevention of alopecia (spot baldness)
- A known antiseptic, good to eat when you have a cold.
- Also thought to be a blood thinner which is good for heart disease

WATERCRESS

NUTRITIONAL INFORMATION

Vitamin A, Vitamin B1 (Thiamin), Vitamin B2 (Riboflavin), Vitamin B6, Vitamin C, Vitamin K, Calcium, Phosphorus, Manganese, Potassium

HEALTH BENEFITS

- Wide range of health benefits being a diuretic, expectorant, hair tonic, digestive, promoter of hunger, stimulant against anaemia, regulator of blood sugar, and to help prevent certain types of cancer
- Increases protection from bacterial and viral infections
- Increases immune function
- Reduces the risk of some cancers including colon cancer
- Offers protection against heart disease
- Aids in alleviation of cardiovascular disease
- Aids in alleviation and protection of high blood pressure
- Aids in protection against Alzheimer's disease
- Aids in the protection against osteoporosis
- Aids in stroke prevention
- Offers antioxidant protection
- Aids in prevention of epileptic seizures
- Can help the prevention of alopecia (spot baldness)

VINE LEAVES

NUTRITIONAL INFORMATION

Vitamin A, Vitamin K, Fibre, Iron, Calcium, Magnesium

HEALTH BENEFITS

- Aids weight control by keeping you feeling fuller
- Aids in cellular development
- Controls blood clotting
- Keeps the skin looking healthy
- Provides antioxidant protection
- Can prevent or slow down varicose veins
- Aids in healthy digestive system
- Keeps teeth and bones strong
- Promotes healthy blood circulation
- Prevents blood sugar spike by releasing sugar slowly into the blood stream

ALMONDS

NUTRITIONAL INFORMATION

Protein, Saturated Fat, Vitamin B1 (Thiamin), Vitamin B2 (Riboflavin), Vitamin B3 (Niacin), Vitamin B9 (Folate, Folic Acid), Vitamin E, Calcium, Dietary Fibre, Magnesium, Phosphorus, Manganese, Iron, Potassium, Copper, Zinc

HEALTH BENEFITS

- Increases immune function
- Can reduce the risk of certain cancers including colon cancer
- Offers protection against heart disease
- Known regulator of blood sugar and insulin dependence
- Slowing in the progression of AIDS
- Slowing in the natural effects of ageing
- Offers DNA repair and protection
- Offers protection against some dementia
- Aids in alleviation of cardiovascular disease
- Offers alleviation and control of high blood pressure
- Known to promote eye health
- Almonds are high in monounsaturated fat which helps to lower blood cholesterol. Half a cup of almonds per day has been shown to lower LDL cholesterol levels by 10%
- Offers protection against Alzheimer's disease
- Aids in the protection against osteoporosis
- Aids in stroke prevention
- Reduces risk of type 2 diabetes
- Reduces frequency of migraine headaches
- Offers alleviation of Premenstrual Syndrome (PMS)
- Offers antioxidant protection
- Aids in the prevention of epileptic seizures
- Offers alleviation of the common cold
- Aids in prevention of alopecia (spot baldness)
- A known anti-inflammatory

OKRA

NUTRITIONAL INFORMATION

Vitamin A, Vitamin B1 (Thiamin), Vitamin B6, Vitamin B9 (Folic Acid), Vitamin C, Vitamin K, Calcium, Magnesium, Phosphorus, Manganese, Iron, Potassium

- Ten essential amino acids
- The mucilage from okra is used to sooth inflammation. Infusions of the pods have been used to treat urogenital problems and chest infections in India
- Offers increased protection from bacterial and viral infections
- Increased immune function
- Reduces the risk of some cancers including colon cancer
- Offers protection against heart disease
- Can slow the natural ageing process
- Offers DNA repair and protection
- Aids in recovery of cardiovascular disease
- Aids in alleviation of high blood pressure
- Offers protection against Alzheimer's disease
- Aids in the protection against osteoporosis
- Aids in stroke prevention
- Reduces the risk of type 2 diabetes
- Reduces the frequency of migraine headaches
- Offers alleviation of Premenstrual Syndrome (PMS)
- Offers antioxidant protection
- Aids in prevention of epileptic seizures
- Aids in prevention of alopecia (spot baldness)

BANANAS

NUTRITIONAL INFORMATION

Vitamin B6, Vitamin B9 (Folic Acid), Vitamin C, Magnesium, Manganese, Potassium

HEALTH BENEFITS

- Increases immune function
- Aids in protection against heart disease
- Slows natural ageing
- Offers DNA repair and protection
- Offers alleviation of cardiovascular disease
- Offers alleviation and control of high blood pressure
- Aids in the protection against osteoporosis
- Offers protection against stroke
- Reduces risk of type 2 diabetes
- Reduces risk of Alzheimer's disease
- Reduces frequency of migraine headaches
- Offers alleviation of Premenstrual Syndrome (PMS)
- Offers antioxidant protection
- Aids in prevention of epileptic seizures
- Aids in prevention of alopecia (spot baldness)

CELERY

NUTRITIONAL INFORMATION

Vitamin A, Vitamin B9 (Folic Acid), Vitamin K, Calcium, Dietary Fibre, Potassium

HEALTH BENEFITS

- Beneficial in the treatment of pain and rheumatism
- Celery is also a popular diet food as it is low in calories and high in fibre
- Increased protection from bacterial and viral infections
- Increases immune function
- Maintains healthy skin
- Reduces the risk of some cancers including colon cancer
- Aids in alleviation of cardiovascular disease
- Offers alleviation and control of high blood pressure
- Aids in the protection against osteoporosis

CINNAMON

NUTRITIONAL INFORMATION

Vitamin A, Vitamin C, Vitamin E, Vitamin K, Calcium, Iron, Magnesium, Zinc, Beta-Carotene, Dietary Fibre.

HEALTH BENEFITS

- A known appetite suppressant
- Highest antioxidant strength in any food
- Reduces risk of type 2 diabetes
- Regulates and reduces blood sugar in diabetics
- Reduces onset of arthritis and osteoporosis
- Antibacterial properties, reducing symptoms of colds, sore throat and cough
- Prevents certain cancers
- Reduces PMS symptoms
- Aids in cognitive function and delays the effects of Alzheimer's disease
- Aids healthy blood circulation, boosting metabolism
- Has anaesthetic properties
- Prevents platelet clogging in blood vessels
- Aids digestion and reduces IBS symptoms
- Protects against coronary heart disease
- Reduces stroke rate
- Controls heart rate and blood pressure

TURMERIC

NUTRITIONAL INFORMATION

Vitamin B3, Vitamin B6, Vitamin C, Vitamin E, Vitamin K, Potassium, Iron, Manganese, Zinc, Calcium, Dietary Fibre

HEALTH BENEFITS

- A known anti-inflammatory
- Found to reduce risk and symptoms of arthritis
- High in antioxidants
- Strengthens immunity, reducing risk of infectious disease
- Controls blood pressure
- Controls bad cholesterol
- Offers protection against some cancers
- Reduces the risk of stroke
- Delays Alzheimer's onset

MILK

NUTRITIONAL INFORMATION

Vitamin A, Vitamin B2, Vitamin B12, Calcium, Potassium, Selenium, Zinc, Magnesium

HEALTH BENEFITS

- Essential for building and maintaining bone and teeth
- Preventative of some cardiac diseases
- Aids in the maintenance of regular blood pressure
- Protects against some types of cancer such as colon cancer
- Reduces the risk of developing type 2 diabetes
- Aids in improving the performance of the nerve system
- Beneficial to growth
- Improves the digestion process
- Boosts natural immunity
- Know to protect eyesight
- Important for maintaining skin, hair, and delicate membranes
- Can treat dehydration
- Provides the body with energy

MINT

NUTRITIONAL INFORMATION

Vitamin A, Vitamin C, Iron, Calcium, Magnesium, Potassium

HEALTH BENEFITS

- Facilitates eye health
- Strengthens immune system
- Protects against some cancers including colon and rectal cancer
- Prevents against cardiovascular disease
- Maintains optimum blood health
- A powerful antioxidant
- Can relieve allergy symptoms
- A natural decongestant
- Calms indigestion
- Aids healthy digestion including relieving pain in IBS sufferers

CUMIN

NUTRITIONAL INFORMATION

Vitamin A, Vitamin B1, Vitamin B2, Vitamin B3, Vitamin B6, Vitamin B9, Vitamin C, Vitamin E, Potassium, Calcium, Iron, Magnesium, Manganese, Phosphorus, Zinc, Beta-Carotene

HEALTH BENEFITS

- Aids in healthy skin
- Has natural anti-ageing properties
- Acts as an antioxidant aiding in prevention of age spots and sagging skin
- Aids lactation for mothers or mothers-to-be
- Lowers blood sugar levels
- Prevents type 2 diabetes
- Reduces anaemia
- Strengthens the immune system
- Aids in healthy menstrual cycle
- Used as some cancer treatments
- Aids in healthy metabolism
- Enzymes break down foods for healthy digestion

MASTIC

HEALTH BENEFITS

- Contains several antioxidants
- Has healing properties
- Has antibacterial properties
- Can ease gastritis and reduce inflammation in the digestive tract
- Lowers cholesterol
- Found to be protective of the liver
- Known to be antiviral
- Found to have anti-cancer properties
- Fights heartburn
- Reduces symptoms of indigestion

CORIANDER

NUTRITIONAL INFORMATION

Vitamin A, Vitamin B9, Vitamin C, Vitamin K, Manganese, Potassium, Calcium

HEALTH BENEFITS

- Clears skin
- Cures diarrhoea
- Beneficial for those suffering with diabetes
- Protects eyes from conjunctivitis
- A known diuretic
- Treats skin inflammation and disorders
- Lowers cholesterol
- Reduces anaemia
- Alleviates of some menstrual disorders
- Regulates blood sugar
- Alleviates hypertension
- Aids bone health
- Known to help cure ulcers

OREGANO

NUTRITIONAL INFORMATION

Vitamin A, Vitamin B1, Vitamin B2, Vitamin B3, Vitamin B5, Vitamin B6, Vitamin B9, Vitamin C, Vitamin K, Iron, Manganese, Beta-Carotene, Dietary Fibre, Zinc, Magnesium, Calcium.

HEALTH BENEFITS

- Controls blood cholesterol
- Aids in sweat production
- Helps gall bladder secretion
- A strong antioxidant
- Controls heart rate and blood pressure
- Strengthens immune function
- Medicinal properties aiding in relief of influenza, fever, indigestion and painful menstruation conditions
- Has anti bacterial properties
- Aids in healthy digestion

Here are a few of my favourite online suppliers…

www.odysea.com
For an amazing selection of wonderful produce.

www.gaea.gr
This company is great. They have a 0-carbon footprint and fantastic produce with a conscience.

www.itshonestlygood.com
For wonderfully good cold pressed Cretan olive oil.

www.hellenicgrocery.co.uk
So many authentic products to choose from.

www.uk.fage.eu
Total Greek yogurt truly is the best, just wonderful yogurt directly from Greece, and we're lucky most supermarkets stock it.

www.greekalicious.nyc
A wonderful supplier of Greek produce & a great fun cookery school based in New York for any American readers.

www.facebook.com/kallonas
For all of you that have watched my shows you will know that this is the BEST rosewater in the world. Even though my uncle has passed, his children are continuing the tradition of making rosewater. They also make beautiful decorative bottles for party favours too – check them out on Facebook.

www.despinafoods.co.uk
This is where I shop for all my Greek and Cypriot ingredients and Kyria Despina makes a mean koupa!

www.myolivebranch.co.uk
Wonderful online suppliers with a great range of Greek produce, from Dakos to olive oil and tapenades to fruit spreads – all delicious!

www.theanamaconcept.com
A wonderful Cypriot sweet wine, which is amazing with cheese, beautifully packaged.

www.antonjewellery.com
You will often see me wearing my chilli earings. I was lucky enough to be sent them and some other beautiful jewellery by the exceptionally talented Steven Milonas who is the creative director of Anton Jewellery (Melbourne).

www.cypressa.co.uk
www.eatgreekflavours.com
www.foodfromcyprus.com
www.atheniangrocery.co.uk
www.ooocompany.com

This is not a food stockist but I am always being asked where I get my dresses from, so here you go: www.theprettydresscompany.com and for an even more retro look: www.dovima.com.

BIBLIOGRAPHY

The Deipnosophists, or Banquet of the Learned by Athenaeus.

The Food Doctor by Vicki Edgson and Ian Marber

The Greek Doctor's Diet by Dr Fedon Alexander Lindberg

Diabetes by Jess Lomas

Greek Eating by Mark Dymiotis

The 10 Secrets to Healthy Ageing by Patrick Holford and Jerome Burne.

Fresh Heather on YouTube and Instagram www.bigcitydreamer.com

Wendy Veale

With years of fun, hard work and experience tucked under my well-worn pinny as a trained home economist, I have worked on food trends and innovation and product development for major food manufacturers as well as create, test and write recipes with tricks of the trade in food styling to top it off – and now I also own The Old School, a lovely Bed and Breakfast in the Cotswolds.

But never too old to learn – for the last ten years I have worked closely with Tonia on the production of Discovery TV's *My Greek Kitchen* series which has meant my tool kit and I have travelled many times to Cyprus and the Greek islands to discover and bring back the most delicious, seasonal and simply prepared recipes I have ever had to taste-test!

Seasonal is key in the Mediterranean and it is a joy to see the freshest, bountiful produce straight from the land or sea, according to the time or year…packed with goodness, simply cooked, with just a few regional ingredients, no fuss, unadulterated, and colourful. I love using my new-found appreciation for Mediterranean cooking skills encompassing its ethos and natural goodness in my Cotswold kitchen.

www.theoldschoolbedandbreakfast.com

Vanessa Courtier

My love of food and all things edible has been my passion and I've had the privilege of working with wonderful chefs and food writers over the years, as photographer, designer or indeed both.

Having travelled to those wonderful Greek markets when working with Tonia on her last book I was totally inspired. 'Taste this, try this…' the flavours of those fresh tomatoes and peppers hooked me completely. So as I roll up my batch of dolmades I think of how Tonia told me how the gossiping women of the village would put the world to rights as they rolled their own dolmades.

It's the way that history, goodness and flavour go hand in hand in the Greek kitchen that makes all these dishes so special for me. Delicious and healthy, what a perfect combination! Thank you Tonia (and Wendy) you're both an inspiration to work with, we are a great team!

www.vanessacourtier.com

Kyprianos Constantinou

Kyprianos Constantinou obtained a Master's degree in Health Psychology at Aston University. He has an understanding of how nutrition contributes to health and behaviour. One of Kyprianos's core belief's is that being healthy is not about how long we live, but about enjoyment of the journey we call life. He believes maintaining a healthy lifestyle is about living to your potential.

Being a fan of Tonia's Greek Kitchen, Kyprianos was attracted to *Eat Greek For a Week*, as he saw it as a fantastic concept that coincided with his beliefs. Tonia's knowledge in the Greek diet is backed up by thousands of years of practice. Furthermore, scientific research is continually conducted to identify the cause of the longer life span and resilience to certain diseases of those living in the Mediterranean when compared to those from the West. Kyprianos believes diet is the contributing variable to the increased health benefits of the Greeks.

To get in touch with Kyprianos Constantinou to discuss anything from your health potential to creating a personalised diet for a specific lifestyles or tastes, you may email him at Maxhealthpotential@gmail.com.

ACKNOWLEDGEMENTS

GOSH THERE ARE SO MANY PEOPLE WHO HAD A HAND IN THIS BOOK, and who I have to thank. First is my wonderful manager Vickie White. She has, over the 14 years I have known her, become much more than a manager, she is my friend, my adviser, she gives me courage and confidence, and sometimes she bullies me! Thank you Vickie for bullying me into writing this book, I am very proud of it.

Of course I would never dream of doing a book without my lovely Wendy Veale. She came with me on my first filming journey to the Greek islands and Cyprus, when I was rather hormonal, as I had literally just had a baby but filming had to start when Zephyros was 10 weeks old; she was there calm and kind. She is so much more than a food economist; she is a food stylist, an editor, always at hand to titivate and correct my terrible grammar! She is totally wonderful. Also in our merry trio is the brilliant Vanessa Courtier. She is an award-winning photographer who has the most wonderful eye for detail. She has written, edited and designed many books of her own and she willingly gave me all her knowledge on this book. These two wonderful English ladies are now honorary Greeks!

I have to say a special thank you to Kyprianos Constantinou for his wonderful nutritional advice and charts. We all know how good the Greek diet is; what is wonderful about Kypros is that he is able to explain the science behind it in a way that we can all understand.

To my publishers Blink who made this book a reality, especially to Clare Tillyer, Joel Simons and Nick Otway, for their patience! To Lisa Hoare, Lizzie Dorney-Kingdom and Tish Tilley, for all their enthusiasm, and to all the team at Blink for being lovely!

A big thank you to the lovely Nabil Mankarious of The Real Greek; I have such fun working on recipes and press events, and special thanks to Christos Karatzenis and Emily Douglas, along with the whole Real Greek team for making coming to work such a joy!

Thank you to my children Antigoni, Sophia, Zephyros and Zeno for being really quite pulchritudinous. I never tell them enough how much I love them but I do, very much. My greatest acknowledgement goes to my husband Paul, without whom I would never have achieved a thing. It has been his unrelenting belief in me and support that has given me the courage to think I can conquer all.

'When a man's stomach is full it makes no difference whether he is rich or poor'

– Euripides